THE

JOSEPH
CAMPBELL

PHENOMENON

THE
JOSEPH
CAMPBELL
PHENOMENON:

IMPLICATIONS
FOR THE
CONTEMPORARY
CHURCH

EDITED BY
LAWRENCE MADDEN

The Georgetown Center for Liturgy, Spirituality and the Arts is an education and research center jointly sponsored by Georgetown University and Holy Trinity Church in Washington, D.C. Through its various workshops, courses and publications, the Center strives to assist American parishes in the continuing work of liturgical renewal.

All scripture quotations are taken from the New American Bible (Catholic Book Publishing Co., 1980).

ISBN: 0-912405-89-9

The Pastoral Press
225 Sheridan Street, NW
Washington, D.C. 20011
(202) 723-1254

The Pastoral Press is the publication division of the National Association of Pastoral Musicians, a membership organization of musicians and clergy dedicated to fostering the art of musical liturgy.

Printed in the United States of America

To the Friends and Benefactors
of
The Georgetown Center for Liturgy, Spirituality,
and the Arts
and in Memory
of
Dr. Benjamin G. Covino

Contents

Introduction

In April 1991 The Georgetown Center for Liturgy, Spirituality and the Arts hosted a conference which presented both an appreciation and a critique of the works of Joseph Campbell, the scholar who popularized the study of mythology in America. Long known in academic circles for such works as *The Hero with a Thousand Faces* and *The Masks of God*, Joseph Campbell was only recently encountered by most Americans in the 1988 six-part television series on PBS hosted by Bill Moyers entitled "The Power of Myth."

The conference was the first sponsored by The Georgetown Center specifically on contemporary American spirituality and its relationship to worship. The response of the more than four hundred participants at the conference was so enthusiastic that more conferences are planned.

The major presentations of that conference are presented here in edited form so that more people may benefit from them. I hope the reader finds as much wisdom in them as I have discovered. Why the person and thought of Joseph Campbell became subjects of such interest to Americans is one of the topics addressed in this volume which features the work of nine scholars from as many disciplines.

Dennis O'Connor, a frequent lecturer on eastern and western wisdom traditions, suggests a way of approaching the material in this volume that will probably yield the most benefit for the individual reader or, better, for the study group that uses it. William Dinges, a specialist in the area of religion and culture, places the Campbell phenomenon in the contemporary American spiritual milieu. Robert Segal examines the relationship between myth and religion in Campbell's thought, and Beverley Zabriskie speaks to Campbell's thought from the point of view of a Jungian analyst. Peter Fink, S.J., a sacramental theologian, presents the results of his personal journey into Joseph Campbell, the man, the scholar and the myth, and Brian McDermott, S.J., a specialist in Christology, explores the myth of Christ's uniqueness and the challenge brought to it in the wake of the Campbell phenomenon. David Steindl-Rast, O.S.B., a monk with extensive experience in the spiritual disciplines of east and west addresses the spiritual challenge Campbell presents to contemporary people. Gertrud Mueller Nelson, an artist, author, and ritualist, explores ways people can celebrate the holy in the ordinary. Finally, Matthew Fox, O.P., well known lecturer and author, outlines the elements of a Christian myth for today's people.

I wish to express my special gratitude to my assistant, Barbara Conley Waldmiller, for her efficient and skillful help in preparing this manuscript and to her computer wiz husband, Ken, for saving the day for us so many times!

Lawrence J. Madden, S.J.

CHAPTER ONE

How Might One Best Use This Book?

Dennis O'Connor

Strive to enter within your inner chamber and you will see the chamber of heaven. For the two are the same and the one entrance leads to both.

St. Isaac of Syria[1]

The plants, rocks, fire, water, all are alive. They watch us and see our needs. They see when we have nothing to protect us, and it is then that they reveal themselves and speak to us.

Morris Edwin Opler[2]

Be patient toward all that is unsolved in your heart and try to love the *questions* themselves like locked rooms and like books that are written in a very foreign tongue. Do not now seek the answers, which cannot be given to you because you would not be able to live them. And the point is to live everything. *Live* the questions now.

Rainer Maria Rilke[3]

How might one best read this book? I suggest we begin by accepting Joseph Campbell on his own terms. I see four crucial dimensions to him.

Accepting Campbell on His Own Terms

First, Joseph Campbell emphasized the experience of life over the intellectual appreciation of its meaning. "People say that what we're all seeking is a meaning for life . . . I think what we're seeking is an experience of being alive, so that our experiences on the purely physical plane will have resonances within our innermost being and reality, so that we actually feel the rapture of being alive."[4] This preference seems consonant with Carl Jung's. "In psychology one possesses nothing unless one has experienced it in reality. Hence a purely intellectual insight is not enough, because one knows only the words and not the substance of the thing from the inside."[5]

Second, as a generalist with a mission, he roamed freely—and without apology—all over the specialists' maps. He saw myths as "stories about the wisdom of life . . . What we're learning in schools is not the wisdom of life. We're learning technologies, we're getting information. There's a curious reluctance on the part of [academic] faculties to indicate the life value of their subjects."[6] Campbell, of course, had no such reluctance. One of his favorite Gnostic texts, The Gospel of Thomas, warns, "If you bring forth what is within you, what you bring forth will save you. If you do not bring forth what is within you, what is within you will destroy you."[7] Ever the extrovert, enthusiast, teacher, and hero returning with the boon of life-giving wisdom, Campbell eagerly shared his inner treasure and the way to find it.

Third, as a comparative mythologist emphasizing similarities over differences, he believed that all heroes were essentially symbolic[8] and that a properly operating mythology served four integrating functions:

> 1. To awaken and maintain in the individual a sense of awe and gratitude in relation to the mystery dimension of the universe, not so that he lives in fear of it, but so that he recognizes that he participates in it as well.
> 2. To offer an image of the universe that will be in accord with the knowledge of the time, the sciences and the fields of action of the folk to whom the mythology is addressed. In our own day, of course, the world pictures of all major religions are at least two thousand years out of date, and in that fact alone there is ground enough for a very serious break-off.

3. To validate, support, and imprint the norms of a given, specific moral order, that, namely, of the society in which the individual is to live.

4. To guide him, stage by stage, in health, strength, and harmony of spirit, through the whole foreseeable course of a useful life.[9]

Fourth, he was a deeply religious person detached from all religious institutional affiliation. I suspect his fierce independence, the verve and missionary zeal of his generalist bent, and his symbolic approach to all religious doctrines obviated confessional membership. Campbell's occasional off-hand remarks are often revealing. "If a person is really involved in a religion and really building his life on it, he better stay with the software he has got. But a chap like myself, who likes to play with the software—well, I can run around, but I will probably never have an experience comparable to that of a saint."[10] When asked during the 1960s who his guru was, he replied, "my guru for the past thirty years has been the Reading Room of the Forty-second Street New York Public Library."[11]

His assiduous meditation practice resembles traditional Christian *lectio divina*. "I meditate by underlining sentences . . . I prefer the gradual path—the way of study . . . Mythic forms reveal themselves gradually in the course of your life if you know what they are and how to pay attention to their emergence. My own initiation into the mythical depth of the unconscious has been through the mind, through the books that surround me in this library."[12]

Approaching Campbell from Many Perspectives

With these four dimensions of Campbell in mind, one may usefully approach this book from many directions. For example, it can be read as a source of information about the man; his influence on contemporary culture and Catholic self-understanding; his relation to myth, cultural history, Jungian thought, and the uses of myth in analytical psychology; his indirect influence on interreligious and intra-religious dialogue; and his popularizing the myth of the hero as central to all myths in every age and culture. This book also witnesses the intellectual and spiritual journeys of several Catholic Christians engaged by the work and example of a deeply religious man who rebelled against authoritarian aspects of the Roman Catholic Church.

Joseph Campbell had many aspects and was received on many different wavelengths. The variety and intensity of these responses recalls the medieval Latin proverb, "whatever is received is received according to the mode of the recipient." He was powerfully experienced as the storyteller recounting Native American myths and medieval romances; the enthusiast praising the glory of Chartres and the riches of Hindu and Buddhist thought and iconography; the iconoclast rejecting religious literalism, cultural parochialism, and absolutist claims by any religious group to have a strangle hold on ultimate Truth; the teacher instructing his students and us to "follow your bliss"; the romantic intellectual adventurer who seemed to embody the values he preached; the professor who criticized academia and was criticized by academic scholars; and the television lecturer who spellbound millions of people who found in him a spiritual guide and inspiration. There is also a disturbing aspect: Campbell has been posthumously accused of being politically reactionary, repressive, and naive, as well as hostile towards women, Jews, black, and gays.[13]

An Invitation to Dialogue

However you approach the text or value Campbell, I would encourage you to enter the spirit of this book by participating in an ongoing, interactive dialogue. Rather than supply ready answers, this volume tends to further your own inquiry and discussion by presenting Campbell from a variety of perspectives, including sociology of religion, mythology, analytical psychology, philosophy, theology, and spirituality. The papers collected in this volume are not meant to be definitive; on the contrary, they presuppose further discussion and questioning. Each piece comes out of a personal struggle to faithfully convey the personal truth that has emerged from research and reflection on very difficult and inevitably controverted questions.

Think of this book, then, as a living text, at once radically open-ended and in need of your contribution. Campbell and the authors have only begun the dialogue; now you can extend and deepen it by exploring new issues and revisiting old ones as you see fit. Each of us enters the dialogue at a unique point. We come with our personal history, temperament, sensibility, learning style, experiences, assumptions, preferences, beliefs, and hopes, our particular interests, urgencies, questions, agenda, biases, blind spots and prejudices, as well as our different levels of receptivity to the issues Campbell raises and the ways he chooses to address them. Where we enter and what we seek may also depend on our familiarity with Campbell's work, our background in the fields he addresses, and our comfort with his presuppositions and methods. And since his field of inquiry is vast (literature, mythology, symbolism, religious experience, philosophy, theology, spirituality, psychology, anthropology, archaeology, ethnography, intellectual and cultural history, etc.) and the volume of his work rather formidable, people will have widely differing responses to both the message and the man presented through his work.

If you are reading this book as part of a study group (which I heartily recommend), you might consider how interdependent learning can foster such dialogue. It differs from traditional styles of learning which are often inherently competitive, promote isolation and anxiety, and reward you for learning by yourself and for yourself. Interdependent learning stresses cooperation over competition and encourages you to learn with, from, and for others in an open-ended process.

If your group is interested in spiritual growth, interdependent learning may involve a recurring pattern of reading, reflection, meditation, questioning, discussion, and return to the texts and the sources. In this way, the process becomes an ever-widening spiral, for as you meditate on a rich text in light of your own experiences and take these issues into your prayer and silence, the text awakens inside your heart, and you being to make innumerable connections. As insights and additional questions arise, you may be moved to share them. And if you go deep enough into the text and listen to it with full attention and an open heart and mind, it may slowly change your vision and behavior. Then you have crossed over from insight into revelation by moving from your mind into your heart, where nourishing change can occur and the deepest Self can grow.

Partners in Dialogue

I imagine as many as five partners in this adventurous dialogue: (1) Campbell; (2) the writer of the particular paper you are currently reading; (3) you the reader; (4) the various sources, figures (historical, mythic, human, divine, etc.) and texts that partners 1, 2, and 3 draw upon to express or interpret their thoughts and feelings in relation to any other member(s) of the dialogue; and (5) the Holy Spirit who dwells in the heart of every person and works unceasingly to illumine us and bring the truth to light. The possibilities for delight and solemn confusion seem promising.

In thinking of how I might help a reader use this book, I imagined a composite fictional person I'll call you. I imagined you had probably seen some portion of the six hours of videotaped discussions with Campbell that Bill Moyers had produced for PBS. Perhaps you've read something by or about Campbell and come armed with impressions, questions, and ideas. Whether you read this book on your own or as part of a group, this is no academic exercise: you're after nourishing truth.

Truth emerges, often as not, from the most unlikely sources: Apache storytellers, lyric poets, or people closer to home and, therefore, more exotic. And truth may face us in the wretched and the dispossessed, the forgotten and the negligible, the displaced and the expendable, the broken and the useless, the "little ones" as Jesus calls them, including those parts of ourselves we have rejected and abandoned in shame or disgust.

Moving from the Mind into the Heart

The three quotations which anchor this discussion suggest a way into the text. Look back at them, if you will, and then calm and quiet yourself, and slowly move from your mind into your heart, as St. Isaac of Syria, one of the desert Fathers, teaches.

Imagine being still as a mountain. Imagine being naked to yourself—unprotected, unrehearsed, uninterpreted. Let the old Apache storyteller's wisdom open you enough to sense that "the plants, rocks, fire, water, all are alive." Draw comfort from your neediness, for thus the world becomes alive and speaks to you.

Until then, it's scenery or appliance, not world—powerful, abiding presence forever addressing you in silence.

Rilke also places us in the heart and urges us to patiently wait in that still center of our being where our energies and faculties are known and integrated. Imagine taking his words to heart. Imagine being patient and trusting enough to go beyond fear and desire and simply wait. Like Mary the mother of Jesus. "And the point is to live everything. Live the questions now." What if we are the question that has to be lived? What would we bring to birth? What divinity waits on us to be born?

"I come that they may have life and have it in abundance." In his paper on "Joseph Campbell's Spiritual Challenge," Br. David Steindl-Rast suggestions that Campbell's emphasis on experiencing aliveness agrees with Jesus's great affirmation in John 10:10. The passage seems to carry both promise and judgment: Your life is empty; I will give you abundant life. If you've lived in words or in things but not in the truth, I'll give you fullness of life. You will no longer be marginal, apart, abstracted, or preoccupied. You will be abundantly alive.

Campbell's life-long interest in the myth of the hero and his sanguine attitude toward death and transformation remind me of a later passage in Rilke:

> We have no reason to mistrust our world, for it is not against us. Has it terrors, they are our terrors; has it abysses, those abysses belong to us....And if only we . . . hold to the difficult, then that which now still seem to us the most alien will become what we most trust and find most faithful . . . [Like] those ancient myths . . . about dragons that at the last moment turn into princesses; perhaps all the dragons of our lives are princesses who are only waiting to se us once beautiful and brave. Perhaps everything terrible is in its deepest being something helpless that wants help from us.[14]

By holding to the difficult and embracing *all* of life on its own sacred terms, we *experience* life in abundance within the mystery of the terrible.

NOTES

1. *Writings from the Philokalia on Prayer of the Heart,* trans., E. Kadloubovsky and G.E.H. Palmer (London: Faber & Faber, 1967) 220.

2. Morris Edwin Opler, *Myths and Tales of the Jicarilla Apache Indians*, Memoirs of the American Folklore Society, vol. 31, 1938, p. 110, cited in Joseph Campbell, *The Hero with a Thousand Faces* 169.

3. Rainer Maria Rilke, *Letters to a Young Poet*, trans., M.D. Herter Norton (New York: W.W. Norton, 1954) 35.

4. Joseph Campbell with Bill Moyers, *The Power of Myth*, paperback ed. (New York: Doubleday, 1988) 5.

5. Carl Jung, *Psychological Reflections: A New Anthology of His Writings, 1905-1961*, eds., Jolande Jacobi and R.F.C. Hull, Bollingen Series XXXI (Princeton: Princeton University Press, 1973) 212.

6. Campbell, *The Power of Myth* 9.

7. Elaine Pagels, *The Gnostic Gospels* (New York: Random House, Vintage, 1981) 143.

8. Scholars have strongly criticized Campbell on this score. See Charles H. Long, "The Dreams of Professor Campbell: Joseph Campbell's *Mythic Image*," *Religious Studies Review* 6 (October 1980) 261-271; Mary R. Lefkowitz, "The Myth of Joseph Campbell," *American Scholar* 59 (Summer 1990) 429-434; and Robert A. Segal, *Joseph Campbell: An Introduction*, rev. ed. (New York: Mentor, 1990).

9. Joseph Campbell, "Schizophrenia—The Inward Journey," *Myths to Live By* (New York: Bantam, 1988) 221-22. This lecture notes that some psychiatrists have credited Campbell's theory of the hero's journey for shedding light on adolescent development and the nature of schizophrenia.

10. Campbell, *The Power of Myth* 20.

11. Reported to me by Dr. Henry Berne.

12. Segal, *Joseph Campbell: An Introduction*, gives this composite quotation, drawn from several published interviews, on p. 22.

13. Tamar Frankiel, "New Age Mythology: A Jewish Response to Joseph Campbell," *Tikkun* 4 (May-June 1989) 23-29; Brendan Gill, "The Faces of Joseph Campbell," *The New York Review of Books* 36 (September 28, 1989) 16-19; "Joseph Campbell: An Exchange," *The New York Review of Books* 36 (November 9, 1989), 57-61; George Rebeck, "Unmasking Joseph Campbell: Hero or TV Charlatan?" *Utne Reader*, (April 1990) 38; and Segal, *Joseph Campbell: An Introduction* 23, 24, and throughout.

14. Rilke, *Letters to a Young Poet* 69.

CHAPTER TWO

Joseph Campbell and the Contemporary American Spiritual Milieu

William D. Dinges

This chapter situates the "Joseph Campbell phenomenon" in the context of the spiritual and religious dimensions of contemporary American culture. The need to contextualize ideas in a broader cultural framework derives from the serpentine character of thought, social structure, and human history. Joseph Campbell belonged to the class of intellectual denizens who produce cultural knowledge. However, the production and dissemination of cultural "knowledge" never occurs in a vacuum; it occurs in the context of a historic *Zeitgeist,* in relationship to modes and dynamics of discourse, to cultural mechanisms of legitimation, and to social class, gender, and ethnic exigencies and orientations.[1] To both appreciate and understand the power and appeal of ideas, especially those of someone who has achieved cultural status (or bane) as a "popularizer," attention must be given to the broader context in which this particular pattern of discourse and knowledge has emerged. As is often the case, it is the context rather than the content that earmarks the significance of an individual's thought, certain ideas acquire cultural currency in one era that they lacked in another. The question is why?

The Joseph Campbell Phenomenon

What is the "Joseph Campbell phenomenon"? In a nutshell, it is the cultural dissemination of the ideas of a comparative mythologist who taught for nearly thirty-seven years in relative obscurity—aside from the academic world and an avid circle of friends and admirers. Although Campbell's first major book (*The Hero with a Thousand Faces*), published in 1949, was followed by a steady stream of popular and scholarly works on mythology, his cultural apotheosis did not occur until the last several decades of his life. Within a year of his death in 1987 at age eighty-three, Campbell was being lionized as the western world's "foremost authority" on mythology," as the "Carl Sagan" of comparative mythographers,[2] as a "sage"[3] and gifted generalist offering new possibilities for the contemporary understanding of myth along with new avenues for spiritual and psychological self-fulfillment.

Campbell's 1988 six-part series with Bill Moyers aired on PBS (edited from twenty-four hours of conversations taped during 1985 and early 1986) drew over 2.5 million viewers each week. The book form of the program (*Power of Myth*) remained on the *New York Times* best-seller list for more than twenty weeks.[4] Campbell's taped lectures on myth have also been widely disseminated in college and university courses on the subject and have become a PBS staple with proven fund-raising effectiveness.

Aside from discussions of his work within academic circles, Campbell's ideas have also been culturally diffused indirectly through film-maker George Lucas' immensely popular "Star Wars" trilogy, through popular literary works like Richard Adams' *Watership Down*, and through conferences, workshops, journals, and other forms of "networking" associated with the spread of the Human Potential movement and "New Age" religiosity.

In short, the Joseph Campbell "phenomenon" points both to the public admiration of a talented and energetic thinker, scholar, lecturer, and teacher, and to the contemporary rehabilitation of myth, especially in terms of its meliorative function (like that of art and religion) as a "stabilizing illusion" central to personal health and societal well-being. Unlike other scholars whose study of mythology has remained largely confined to academic circles (e.g., Eliade, Levi-Strauss), Campbell's images and ideas now animate much of the broader public discourse on the hero's journey, shamanism, mother goddesses, notions of sacred space, and self-realization.[5] Campbell's books and lectures also continue to con-tribute to the ongoing religious megasynthesis of east and west by popularizing religious symbols and ideas associated with various eastern esoteric psychologies, philosophies, and religious traditions.

Through his writings and public appearances, Campbell brought both a recovery of and heightened sensibility to the meaning of myth as a form of cultural language and thought. However, while he did not start a religious or therapeutic movement, Campbell's thinking on mythology is clearly more than a purely literary or academic exercise. For Campbell, myths are clues to our deepest spiritual potentials. They express "controlled and intended statements of certain spiritual principles, which have remained constant throughout the course of human history."[6] In evangelic-like fashion, Campbell preached the gospel of myth as the truest guide to understanding human experience. He asserted, in essence, that myth had the power to bring us to where we are brought by religion: to inward illumination, to an experience of ultimate meaning beyond the bounds of ordinary certainties and knowledge, to the fullest potentiality of personhood, to an experience of heightened consciousness from which vitality flows. Focus on the "Joseph Campbell phenomenon" is, therefore, highly relevant to any discussion of the ongoing realignment of religion and culture in American society and to the nature and meaning of spirituality and self-realization as we begin our turn toward the new millennium.

Campbell's current public visibility and media acclaim notwithstanding, a few cautionary notes are in order. To begin with, we do not, in fact, know the actual scope of the "Campbell phenomenon." While the number of books and videos sold may be some indication of the extent of his following, the number of people who have actually read the corpus of his work (which is formidable) and actually incorporated the variegated meaning of the "power of myth" into their own spiritual lexicon or *Weltanschauung* remains unknown.

Second, even if we accept the "phenomenal" character of Campbell's appeal, its long-term holding power in the American cultural and spiritual imagination remains to be seen. Among the ever shifting mores, status symbols, and appetites of middle-class consumption culture, "name recognition" is no antidote to faddism. Nor is it a guarantor of long-term shelf-life. The Moyers' program was Campbell's first real exposure to the mass American public.[7] However, we are all aware of the quicksilver nature of media-derived public affection. My own suspicion is that Campbell's appeal remains confined primarily to the inner-directed and affluent cultural left, to serial spiritual experimenters, and to cultural cosmopolitans and academic elites—although many of his ideas on mythology will continue to move through the culture at large via mass media channels (lectures, video tapes, audiocassettes, etc.).[8]

Third, not everyone finds Campbell's myth-as-mega-religion idea intellectually sound or spiritually edifying. With a few exceptions (including some reviews of his books), Campbell's thought has yet to run the full Ph.D. gauntlet, or come under other forms of rigorous academic scrutiny—although some critical assessments have emerged in recent years. To date, this criticism has focused on Campbell's assertions regarding the essential sameness of all religio-mythic systems, on inconsistencies in his thought, on his sexism (in spite of his popularization of feminine goddesses), his cultural parochialism, and his tendency to treat myths outside their concrete historical situation.[9]

Nor has Campbell's "power of myth" struck a responsive cord among the ranks of American's forty-to-fifty-million-plus "Bible believing Christians" who do not separate "faith" from "church," who do not read the Bible as "myth," who do not believe that inner spirituality is self-generated, who are not partial to religious syncretism, and who see in the Human Potential and New Age movements signs of "neo-paganism" and "false religion" that contaminate the "true" faith and mark an apostate age. Indeed, it is indicative of the current fault line in American religious life that Campbell's symbolic, syncretistic, and "world ecumenist" perspective[10] has come to the fore collaterally with the revival of conservative and fundamentalist religious traditions that make absolute and exclusive claims and that abide unabashedly by a literal interpretation of a sacred text.

The above caveats notwithstanding, let me now turn to the subject at hand, situating the "Joseph Campbell phenomenon" in the broader context of American spiritual and religious culture.

Culture Crisis

As I noted in the introduction, the first point of interest regarding Joseph Campbell's appeal, both as a comparative mythologist and as a publicly proclaimed free lance spiritual seer, is the historical context in which he achieved this status. Although Campbell had been producing scholarly works on mythology for some time, his public popularity emerged largely in the wake of the "culture crisis" upheaval in American life that began in the 1960s.

The "Age of Aquarius" that commenced with Camelot and that ended with the nightmare at the Altamont raceway in California was a traumatic and wrenching period in American history. It was a time during which the transition into a post-Puritan, post-Protestant, post-Christian era accelerated dramatically.[11] The scope of this "culture crisis" included the demise of American Civil Religion,[12] the erosion of the legitimacy of the American way of life, and widespread cynicism regarding the efficacy of the "American dream." The Sixties were a time of conflict and oddity marked by the clenched fist, by urban rioting and campus violence, by assassinations and civil unrest, by a "Generation Gap," by the "Other America" and a failed "War on Poverty," by disdain for the "Establishment," by a bitter civil rights struggle and a morally bankrupt war, and by anti-institutionalism and antinomian "counterculture" radicalism. Taken collectively, the social, political, and cultural turmoil of the 1960s signaled a significant break with much of the shared meaning and symbolism of the American past.[13] Few institutions were left untouched by this cultural convolution and attendant crisis of legitimation, least of all those "soft" or "mediating" structures concerned with religion and human motivation.[14]

The noteworthy aspect of the "culture crisis" era and its aftermath that I want to highlight here was the decline of the "mainline religions" (Protestant, Catholic, Reform and Conservative Judaism) that historically constituted the numerical bulk of church-going America. These traditions had long exercised cultural hegemony and had been a core source of meaning, morality, and social solidarity in American society. By the latter 1960s, however, it had become clear that they were losing both membership and cultural vitality—trends that continued through the 1970s and 1980s.[15]

Why the mainline declined has been the subject of considerable debate.[16] Some observers have noted the link between their decline and the broader cultural weakening of liberalism, that synthesis of rational religion and humanism that had long held sway over the middle ground in American society.[17] Others saw the decline stemming from the lack of discipline and certainties within the mainline churches themselves and/or due to the "culture religion" syndrome to which they had become captive.[18] (Campbell asserted that the decline was attributable to the message of the mainline itself. The mythology of the Christian tradition, he claimed, was profoundly "out of date."[19])

The point I wish to emphasize here, however, is not the cause of the decline of the mainline, but the fact that in its wake, many young, well-educated, and affluent Americans (whose numbers had been increasing dramatically during the period under consideration) became "unchurched" and spiritually adrift. Furthermore, many of those who remained within their traditions found themselves embroiled in bitter internecine conflicts over issues of change and authority. These issues included the allocation of resources, doctrinal agendas surrounding ordination, homosexuality, abortion, the legitimacy of the Charismatic movement and feminist spirituality and theology, "peace and justice" issues, the question of how to interpret the Bible, and matters of liturgical practice and renewal.[20] These internal conflicts, in turn, reflected the widening divisions and tensions that had been fermenting for some time within denominations between religious liberals and religious conservatives.

In addition to the travails of the Nation's mainline "sacred canopy," another aspect of the "cultural crisis" also became accentuated in the 1960s. This is the "crisis of unbelief"[21] or, as it is more widely known, the crisis of secularity surrounding domination of the rational, scientific, technical and instrumental over the moral, humanistic, and emotional. This "crisis of unbelief" (currently discussed under the rubric of "post-modernism") has been present in western culture for some time. In essence it points to the insufficiencies of scientism, scientific materialism, and instrumental behaviorism in resolving the existential problems of our day. It refers to the spiritual poverty of a life-world dominated by massive bureaucracy, aesthetic sterility, and pure technical order. It also refers to the tragedy of sacrificing the whole person to one of their parts, and to the climate of depersonalization and coercion characterizing large portions of modern life. And, like the crisis of the mainline decline, the "crisis of unbelief" also has a specific social location among the affluent and upper middle-class.

However, while it is true that there has been a decline in religious involvement among those affected by the crisis of belief and unbelief, and an attendant decline in the influence of traditional religion relative to that of other social institutions,[22] there is little indication that the majority of individuals have become hardened materialists or that they have atrophied spiritually or brought their quest for spiritual validation to a halt.[23]

To the contrary, the "culture crisis" era has been a period of widespread religious effervescence and spiritual innovation in American society. New religious movements proliferated in the late 1960s and early 1970s (followed by a strong recovery of identity and cultural assertiveness on the religious right during the 1970s and 1980s). Religious experimentation in the guise of "consciousness raising," quasi-religious holistic health movements, and self-help therapies also became widespread in the last three decades as has interest in meditation, spiritualism, astrology, and myth. Indeed, the concept of "religious pluralism" along with the very definition of "religion" itself have accrued entirely new meanings in American society since the 1960s.[24] This situation has led any number of historically-minded observers to characterize the period as a Third or Fourth (depending on how one counts) "Great Awakening" in the American religious experience.[25]

In spite of the holding power of belief in the allegedly intractable character of secularization, the desire for ultimate meaning, self-knowledge, inner peace, and a sense of cosmic order have not evaporated for most individuals. As Roof and McKinney have noted, even among the unchurched, the evidence suggests that these individuals are overwhelmingly believers and quite religious in many respects—although they hold less conventional values and express their religion apart from churches.[26] While those on the religious right reaffirmed a "fundamentalist" defense in the face of cultural crisis and spreading secularism, many of those on the cultural and religious left embarked upon new spiritual journeys and experiments. They did so either by reappropriating traditional symbols and rituals thereby giving them more relevant meaning and experiential significance, or by seeking to find meaning and significance in entirely new ones derived from non-western and esoteric traditions.[27] The popularity of Joseph Campbell's perspective on mythology with its elevation of myth as a new (yet old) type of spiritual and psychological capital from which enlightenment and personal well-being can be derived, needs to be situated, first and foremost, in this broader context of cultural upheaval, spiritual hypochondria, and the dynamics of religious revitalization and experimentation.

What I am posing here is a "vacuum theory" approach to the renewed interest in mythology in general and to the appeal of Joseph Campbell in particular. The collapse of the Enlightenment dream of the rationalist millennium has left a spiritual void in contemporary culture. This void, in turn, has provided inducement for movements of counter-secularity, for a re-enchantment of the universe, for the taking up of vestiges of ancient myths, for an elevation of the sacred and expressive side of life over the purely rational and instrumental, for new schemes of coherence and meaning, and for new avenues of spiritual and psychological self-fulfillment. The social and spiritual traumas associated with the inner decay of American culture and its religious traditions over the last three decades, combined with the free-market nature of the American religious economy, have proven highly conducive to the rise of and receptivity to new religious movements and metaphysical orientations, to the emergence of new symbol systems, to the search for a "new story" in human experience, and to a rediscovery of the transcendent and of new modalities for self-fulfillment. During a time of cultural and social upheaval, when conventional religious symbol systems lost much of their evocative power and cultural authority, especially among the more affluent social classes, Joseph Campbell's vision of the "power of myth" offered the possibility of a new template, a new path for spiritual revitalization and for the experience of "transcendence." Campbell's thinking also harmonized with the emerging "New

Age" initiative to reconnect with the ancient insights and wisdom of the past. Furthermore, Campbell offered to the better educated who carried with them a more liberal cultural and religious orientation a highly individualized path to self-realization, one that was unencumbered by dogmatism, by institutional demands, by any system of morality, or by the necessity of a community commitment.

Like Rudolf Bultmann with whom he has been compared(but whom he repudiated for holding to a "literalist" interpretation of the resurrection[28]), Campbell also recognized that modern science had rendered void many of the great myths and symbolic universes though which the individual gained personal and social meaning. And, like Bultmann, Campbell encouraged the pursuit of functional substitutes ("creative mythology") to facilitate access to these "ancient truths."[29]

The New Religious Consciousness

While the appeal of Campbell's gospel of myth can be situated within this "culture crisis" scenario, much of what he expounded on the "power of myth" was also congruent with broader cultural and theological shifts attending the rise of the Aquarian "new religious consciousness," a phenomenon that metamorphosed into the "New Age" movement by the late 1970s.

As I indicated earlier, this "new religious consciousness" was, itself, part of a deeper cultural malaise. It had roots in early 1960s ("death of God") theological radicalism, in an emerging "new morality," and in the growth of a psychedelic drug culture in which mystical experience, once the prerogative of saints and seers, now became readily available to nearly everyone.[30] The diffusion of eastern religions through the emergence of "religious studies" programs and through increased Asian immigration over the last three decades also facilitated the spread of the "new religious consciousness."[31] What, then, were some of the affinities between Joseph Campbell's thinking on mythology, self-discovery, and spiritual growth and this emerging "new religious consciousness"?

To begin with, the "new religious consciousness" was hallmarked by an opposition to wooden dogmatism and creedal formulas, to code morality, to ritual formalism, and to sterile rational and instrumental values. The spiritual effervescence of the 1960s highlighted the Post-Reformation conviction that reason was of limited use as a determinant of religious truth. While it is true that some of the new religions associated with the "new religious consciousness" did construct theological edifices, their central appeal derived from their emphasis on the primacy of "experience," of visceral values, of a subjective, feeling-oriented religiosity that paralleled the "ecstatic radicalism" that had characterized the more flamboyant elements of the 1960s hippie counter-culture.[32] This "ecstatic spiritualism" could be found in forms as diverse as "Charismatic" glossolalia, A.C. Bhaktivadanta's "Krishna consciousness," and the resurgence of hasidic Judaism. In addition, Gallup polls were reporting by the mid-1970s that one out of every three Americans had some type of "born again" religious experience. Roman Catholics, in particular, came to discover in the Age of Aquarius the spiritual fecundity of "religious experience," that once forbidden fruit long-tainted in the church as a "Protestant" and or "modernist" phenomenon.

Campbell's message on the "power of myth" likewise played heavily on the experiential, affective, and symbolic aspects of life and spirit while deprecating the role of ideology, doctrines, dogma, and institutional religious authority. Campbell, like the artistic poetic geniuses he so admired, extolled action and imagination over rational thought. He maintained that myth expresses "raw, unfiltered experience" and that myth can only be "experienced."[33] The true power of myth lay precisely in its "affect value."[34] Campbell's writings consistently elevate the shaman and artist (whose authority derived from experience) over the priest, the "functionary," the custodian of facts and forms, the person of the book.[35] Unlike theology, which springs from the "dicta of authority," creative mythology flows from "the insights, sentiments, thought, and vision of an adequate individual loyal to his own experience of value."[36] As more than one commentator has noted, Campbell's disdain for theologians and his critique of western theology (and western religion in general) derived from its penchant for creed and dogma and abandonment of poetic language and the authority of experience, its tendencies to "demythologize," to change metaphors into historical fact and poetry into prose. According to Campbell, these tendencies led to divisiveness and the unwarranted validation of a particular social order as divinely ordained.[37] Campbell tersely summed up his own position regarding the spiritual priority of experience when he told Bill Moyers that he did not need faith because "I have experience."

Campbell's adulation of "experience" as the genesis of spiritual and mythopoetic truth resonated well with the countercultural celebration of affectivity and the resurgence of experiential and "ecstatic spiritualism" that earmarked the "New Light" religious enthusiasm of the last three decades. Collaterally, his disdain for institutional religious authority—which he articulated with particular vigor in a 1968 article on "The Secularization of the Sacred"[38]—also mirrored the anti-institutionalism and rebellion against old authorities by many of the Baby Boomer generation whose core youth experience included a Jacobin-like disdain for "the Establishment"—religious and otherwise.

Second, and closely related to the above, the "new religious consciousness" also gave expression to a growing interest in mysticism, in the various technologies of prayer, meditation, and "higher consciousness," in the discovery that "the Kingdom of God is within" or that "All is One." The boom in oriental meditation religions, the "chemical contemplation" of the psychedelic era,[39] the proliferation of ashrams, prayer and retreat centers and popular and academic works on Ti Chi, Zen, Tantra, "peak experiences," and various meditation techniques were among the more conspicuous indications of a widening hunger for mystical experience in the American population.[40] Noteworthy, too, in this regard was the fact that by the early 1970s, many of the Esalen-style encounter and Human Potential movements (Primal Therapy, Arica, Silva Mind Control, various gestalt groups) that were mushrooming across the United States were also becoming less psychoanalytic and more mystical in their therapeutic approach[41] borrowing, for instance, chanting and meditation techniques from Buddhist, Hindu, and in some cases, Christian traditions. The scope of the interest in mysticism and "peak experience" in the post-1960s era was also suggested by Gallup and other large scale sociological surveys pointing to widespread experimentation in this regard, especially among the better-educated and privileged strata of society.[42]

Campbell's message on the "power of myth" likewise emphasized myth's relatedness to mystical awareness and inward spiritual potential. Campbell asserted that the true spiritual order lies within the person and nature, that ultimate reality is here and now, that there are "no gods out there that are not right here . . ."[43] Accordingly, myth offers mystical possibilities for the release of spiritual energies that are internally derived. The "inexhaustible and multifariously wonderful divine existence" of which we are constituted is to be found not among the planets or beyond or in the tribe, race, continent, or social class, but within the mystical depths of the individual.[44] For Campbell, the very essence of myth was its mystical message describing mind and cosmos. As Professor Segal has noted, however, Campbell's mysticism was one that espoused self-reliance rather than self-effacement[45]—a point to which I will return later.

Third, the "new religious consciousness" and its "New Age" progeny promoted a highly eclectic and syncretistic spirituality that drew heavily on non-western and non-Christian traditions.

The appeal of religious syncretism that has been growing steadily in the west over the last several decades is related to the great age of "dialogue" emerging after World War II, to the weakening of pressures for religious conformity, to difficulties of maintaining absolutistic religious claims in a pluralistic and relativistic cultural milieu, and to the growing awareness of global spirituality in our time. This development is also linked to trends in contemporary American religion, notably the declining significance of denominationalism and narrowly defined religious interest and identity (although these latter tendencies continue unabated in conservative and fundamentalist traditions).

As a comparative mythologist, Campbell's approach to spiritual truth was also highly syncretistic, reflecting his own conviction of a "universal" mytho-poetic heritage. It mattered not to Campbell that one's guiding angel is named Vishnu, Jesus, or the Buddha because, "the same message is there, variously turned."[46] Conversely, Campbell berated the "ethnocentric historicism" of the Judeo-Christian tradition with its idea of uniqueness and exclusivism. He rejected all "one truth" authoritarianism emanating from organized religion. According to Campbell, "the exclusivism of there being only one way in which we are saved, the idea that there is a single religious group that is the sole possessor of truth, that is the world as we know it, and that must pass away."[47] Campbell saw the "new condition of humanity" as one of progress, humanism, democracy, science and world ecumenism. He espoused the broader cultural ethos of relativism and asserted that the thrust of modern science had been to show decisively that in the moral realm, "there is no single human norm."[48] Nor within this relativized world-cultural context was there anything unique or distinctive about Christian imagery or symbolism; Christianity was simply another culturally and historically conditioned mode for expressing something about the divine within. Given its tendencies toward "dogmatic and historicizing theology,"[49] its "outdated" mythology, and its "Lavantine assurance of a separation of spirit and nature,"[50] Campbell found it severely wanting.

Other Cultural Convergences

In addition to the "cultural crisis" that opened new vistas for spiritual revitalization and in addition to the symmetry of some of the core themes of Campbell's thinking on mythology with an emerging "new religious consciousness," other aspects of his thought were also in keeping with broader cultural trends antecedent to the 1960s.

Psychology as Religion

In its Jungian affinities, Campbell's thinking on myth which heavily emphasizes a mystical and psychological interpretation, perpetuates other twentieth-century tendencies toward the convergence of religion and psychology (or what some see as the "triumph" of psychology over religion). In this situation the therapist (mythologist) acts as a surrogate theologian and psychology (mythology) becomes a language of faith; here also psychotherapy (mythic symbolism) provides the functional equivalent of the therapeutic effect of Christian imagery and institutions.

Philip Rieff, one of the more articulate critics of this development, has pointed out that in the wake of the historical fragmenta-

tion of Christianity, many educated Christians have been searching for more purely symbolic sources to which they could transfer
their loyalty and authority. "Biblicism gave way to erudition,
erudition to historical liberalism, and the latter to a variety of
psychological conservatisms . . ."[51] In the context of this development, outright hostility to religion has been displaced by a more
sympathetic view of the need for mythic explanations and the
conviction that religious assertions need only be taken seriously
insofar as they are a symbol of something else.[52] This psychologized religiosity has deeply penetrated contemporary American
religion. As Wuthnow has observed, while a high degree of
supernaturalism remains as a formal tenet of belief for many
Americans, the operational relevance of the supernatural has in
many respects collapsed into the interior concerns of the self.[53] This
reflects, again, the broader dissolution of the idea that God is "out
there."

Campbell's message on the "power of myth" belongs in this
same line of intellectual pedigree in which Jung plays such a
seminal role. Myth provides for Campbell as it did for Jung a key
to unlocking deep psychic treasures. These treasures are interpreted as manifestations of spiritual truths. Myth now functions as
a mode of religious psychology for much of what formerly was
offered by the Christian tradition in modern western culture. Myth
enables the theologically disenchanted to find the "lost God" of
their time not in the above or beyond, but in the below and within.[54]
Thus, like Jung, Campbell has unveiled through the genre of myth
an imaginative discourse of spirituality, but one that is highly
psychologized and "without the bother of churches or the imposi-
tion of consequential ethics."[55] From Campbell's perspective, when
the "Kingdom comes," it does so in terms of the individual's inner
psychospiritual resources, not historically and socially.[56]

Campbell's psychologized spirituality focused on the "inward
potential" of the individual and, concerned with individuation
and self-realization, struck a particularly responsive cord in the
cultural climate of the 1970s and 1980s. This was especially so
among those individuals who were increasingly pre-occupied out
of boredom and isolation with their own inner psychological
needs and who became dominated by a therapeutic desire to share
"feelings" and to embark upon the high road of self-discovery and

personal fulfillment.[57] (And, I might add, with the financial where-
withal to do so.) This psychologized religiosity which Campbell
among others helped to popularize, along with various humanistic or human potential techniques and "training," became freely
adopted by many mainline church and parachurch programs in
the 1970s,[58] providing a new modality of religious discourse for the
more culturally and spiritually sophisticated.

In a similar vein, Campbell's work—particularly his popular
study of hero/savior mythology—was also concordant with aspects of the revolution in contemporary cognitive psychology, a
revolution that emphasizes the ability of the individual to become
a more active force in their own life, to set challenges and to make
efforts to meet them.[59] Campbell's perspective on hero/savior
mythology also has affinities with other forms of twentieth-century self-help and self-improvement psycho-religiosity, where
spiritual maturity is linked with physical and mental well-being
and the fulfillment of human growth and potential (e.g., in the
work of James, Allport, Maslow and, more recently, M. Scott Peck
and Robert Schuller).

Cultural Individualism

Another issue bearing on Campbell's popularity concerns the
broader cultural phenomenon of individualism in American society. Here, however, the question of the affinity between ideas and
cultural trends is less clear.

During the Reagan era, when Campbell leaped into public
fame, a new surge of heightened individualism swept the country
along with the unabashed adulation of greed, conspicuous consumption of the affluent, widespread abandonment of civic virtue,
and a widening discrepancy between America's haves and have
nots. During this same period, the "new religious consciousness"
of the 1960s completed its transformation into the "New Age"
movement of the 1980s. The "Moral Majority" rose and fell as did
a number of well-known televangelists implicated in highly pub-
licized sexual and financial scandals. Furthermore, many of the
transformative tasks that preoccupied the "do-yourself-a-favor-
today" crowd during the 1970s such as the search for community,
rethinking personal goals, becoming "self-actualized," re-tooling

the "self," and fulfilling one's "human potential"[60] along with crasser forms of spiritual self-indulgence and cultural narcissism continued unabated throughout the 1980s. (As Tom Wolfe had noted earlier, the promised "transformation" of the Age of Aquarius was slow in coming!)

The question here is what (if any) link exists between Campbell's growing popularity in the 1980s and these wider cultural developments?

Clearly, Campbell's "power of myth" cannot be linked directly with the greed and avarice that earmarked the era. Throughout his writings, Campbell made clear that the hero-savior journey is a psychological and spiritual process, not one characterized by the pursuit of material greed as symbolized by Gordon Gekko in the movie "Wall Street." In Campbell's scheme the true hero-savior is one who brings forth a richer and more mature psychological/ spiritual condition, one who gives his/her life to "something bigger" than themselves.[61]

However, while not implicated directly to greed and wanton pursuit of materialism, the implication of Campbell's "power of myth" is more problematic in relationship to the cultural shift toward greater self-aggrandizement, heightened individualism, and the quest for the ideal "self" that earmarked much of the 1970s and 1980s. The link here, according to some critics, is to be found in one of the *leit motifs* in Campbell's hero/savior monomyth and, even more directly, in what is perhaps Campbell's best-know signature phrase, "follow your bliss." This spiritual aphorism faintly echoes the Army's call to "be all that you can be" and/or that hackneyed counter-culture phase of the 1960s, "do your own thing."

With regard to the hero/savior monomyth, the true hero according to Campbell (personified par excellence by Wolfram von Eschenbach's Parzival), relies only on himself, following his own direction and no one else's. Closely linked to this conceptualization of the self-reliant "hero" is the idea that authentic meaning today cannot be derived from the group, but can be found only in the "self-expressive individual"[62] whose creative style is "not dissolution but individuation, and who will be nobody's victim."[63] For Campbell, the true cultural and spiritual heroes are those "giants of creative thought" who have emancipated themselves from the "matrix of inherited social bondages . . ."[64] Indeed, Campbell argued repeatedly from the late 1950s on that the emergence of the heroic individual in passionate pursuit of their own self-actualization and relying on their own experience and authority, has been one of the greatest cultural innovations of western society.[65]

What, precisely, Campbell meant by the dictum "follow your bliss," and the values implicit in doing so have been the subject of considerable debate. Brendan Gill writing in the September 28, 1989, issue of the *New York Review of Books* criticized Campbell for his political naiveté and for propagating a message that, while appearing to promote liberal thinking, especially that regarding the challenge to institutionalized authority (religious, political, cultural), simultaneously conveyed self-serving and self-indulgent themes. From Gill's perspective, Campbell's bliss-following hero is but another version of the quintessential rugged individualist whose primary concern is the chimerical pursuit of "happiness." Campbell seemed to reinforce this interpretation when he told Bill Moyers that "following your bliss" is about "staying with" whatever makes you happy.[66]

Although it is true that Campbell had been singing the praises of following one's "bliss" long before he became a cultural icon in the 1980s, it is not hard to imagine why the call to "stay with whatever makes you happy" would find a receptive audience during that particular decade, especially among those whose exposure to Campbell had only come through the medium of television and who were, for the most part, unfamiliar with the larger corpus of his work wherein such advice needed properly to be situated. In addition, Campbell's message accentuating the role of the individual in pursuit of his or her "bliss" also resonated well with the political disenchantment of the time.

By the 1980s, the conviction that social engineering by human minds, technical skills, and financial resources could solve major social problems had lost considerable credibility. The self-fulfillment crowd of the 1980s included within its ranks no small number of activist casualties of the 1960s who had abandoned many of their youthful fantasies of instant political and cultural transformation. Having discovered the "Aquarian Conspiracy," many now worked from the assumption that it was not class, race, or gender that mattered as causal factors in social outcomes, but internal *individual* initiatives for change and self-improvement.[67] Campbell's thought reinforced this political naiveté in a number of ways, notably by his well-know disdain for "utopian" visions, his assertion that on the "metaphysical plane" good and evil were essentially indistinguishable,[68] and by the argument that individuals were essentially to blame for their own shortcomings in life.[69]

As Yankelovich had noted, by the 1980s the graying "Me Decade" generation had turned the self-denial ethic on its head by advocating the strange moral principle that the individual had a "duty to themselves" and that self-knowledge is its own reward. The call to "follow your bliss" was, therefore, quite appropriately a fitting benediction for what one social critic called "the greatest age of individualism in American history."[70] This was, after all, an era that had spawned a host of publishing gems promoting personal aggrandizement (e.g., *Looking out for Number One, How to be Your Own Best Friend, Pulling Your Own Strings*).[71] It was also a period that saw the full flowering of the Human Potential movement and a montage of self-help and self-improvement groups that promised "transformation" and success for those individuals who would only "take responsibility" for their lives.

Campbell's public pronouncements did little to clarify the meaning of "follow your bliss," just as he tended to neglect, in general, the broader discussion of the social function of myth. (How, for instance, was the advice to "follow your bliss" related to moral guidance or to the larger social scheme of things?) The point here is that the dictum to "follow your bliss"—which sounded oddly out of place in the conformist climate of the 1950s—resonated well in the individualist climate of 1980s where political disillusionment ran high and where the notions of public service, corporate responsibility, and social justice were out, while those of greed, personal aggrandizement, and self-fulfillment were in. In a worse case scenario, Campbell's clarion call implicitly sanctioned selfishness and indirectly reinforced the Ayn Rand Gospel of right-wing individualism and anti-humanitarianism. This was the essence of the charge raised by Brendan Gill.[72] In more benign terms, "follow your bliss" was merely an idiom of Campbell's "sentimental side" or, as a friend noted, a "perpetually adolescent" expression of his romantic idealism.[73]

American Romanticism

Aside from any debate over the meaning and the moral and social implications of Campbell's advice to "follow your bliss" and to "stay with whatever makes you happy," his adulation of heroic individualism in pursuit of the Grail of self-enlightenment is also entirely in keeping with the American proclivity to elevate the life of the ordinary person to the status of high drama. It is also an idea that reinforces the quintessential American dream of transcending one's class and background by reinventing one's self. Nor should the connections between Campbell's thinking and the tradition of American romanticism be overlooked. Consider, for example, some of the similarities between Campbell and Ralph Waldo Emerson, another spiritual seer and cultural icon of an earlier era.

Emerson, like Campbell, was influenced by strands of European philosophy, romanticism, and oriental religion. Emerson also held to a brand of "inner light" mysticism, to a this-worldly perspective, to the priority of symbolic modes of interpretation, to the power of imagination, intuition, and emotion over pure intellectualism, and to concern with the vast world of the individual's inner life. Emerson also advocated independence of spirit ("self-reliance"), the exaltation of the personal conscience above human law and tradition, the apotheosis of the individual, and the necessity of one's mission to realize divine capabilities that lay within the self and nature, not in some life after death or celestial hinterland. Emerson also deplored the American obsession with the purely practical and expressed disdain for those Babbitt-like philistines who did no more than work for a living and who lacked the willingness and heroism to sacrifice everything for their dreams or, in Campbell's terms, who failed to "follow their bliss." Finally, Emerson, like Campbell portrayed great faith in the historic (and mythic) role of the hero of whom history was but the lengthened shadow.

In his role as a contemporary exemplar of the romantic tradition, Campbell's appeal may be viewed as a response to the stultification of the individual that characterizes much of the contemporary culture of managerial capitalism dominated by bureaucracy and instrumental rationality. For many individuals, modern society has caused a feeling of not being truly alive, a sense of impotence and ennui; it has dulled people's conviction that life is in some way a great adventure, that it is something to be embraced fully and not merely passively endured, that it is not a series of dangers to be avoided.[74] Campbell's message on the "power of myth," by contrast, calls for an embrace of the fullness of life and the gamut of human experience. Campbell, himself, exuded personal vitality and a deep passion for living. He exemplified the conviction that the answer to the riddle of life lay in the living of life itself, in the fullness of its diversity and in its hope and terror. As he put it: "The spiritual is really the bouquet of life."[75]

Spiritual Individualism

The movement toward heightened individualism in the cultural and psychological sphere that characterized much of the 1970s and 1980s also spilled over into American religious life during the same period. Campbell's message on the "power of myth" is highly relevant to this development, and in a manner that is more direct and apparent than in the matter of his message's ambiguous relationship to the emerging culture of narcissism.

As I noted earlier, one of the major developments of the post-1960s era has been the tendency toward greater religious privatization and individualism. This privatization has been manifest in a variety of ways with the overall thrust, as John Wilson has noted, being that of transforming divine commandments "into instrumental strategies for achieving personal satisfaction."[76] This tendency toward religious privatization, closely linked to the psychologizing of religion à la Jung and others, discussed earlier, reflects the broader fragmenting of life in the late twentieth century and the cultural diffusion and increasing differentiation of religion associated with secularity.[77] Highly privatized religion (dubbed "Sheilaism" by Bellah and his colleagues in *Habits of the Heart*) has also been attended by what Durkheim called the "cult of the individual," a cultural ethos in which personal psychological, emotional, social, and spiritual needs take precedence over inherited ties to a normative community.[78]

There is, of course, a long standing religious tradition calling for the individual to establish their own spiritual authority (Campbell's thinking is hardly unique in this regard). In the

American experience, however, religious individualism has been amplified by a powerful cultural mythology that extols self-reliant and expressive individualism while heightening the fear of any kind of dependency.[79] Traceable in more recent times to the priorities of the 1960s emphasis on individual choice and moral pluralism, religious privatization and the attendant spiritual individualism became full-blown by the 1980s.[80] Although it is true that some individuals were led into religious communities in the post-1960s era as a result of "finding themselves," many, in fact, were not. Religion in the American mainstream has become increasingly relegated to the purely private realm and, therefore, largely "invisible" vis-à-vis the larger society.[81] The consequences of this "shrinking" of church religion are numerous: faith and spirituality are removed from a community and institutional basis, denominational loyalties are weakened, and a common moral vocabulary evaporates. Religion is reduced to the purely subjective dimension of individual "opinion," "taste," or "preference." Religion also loses its force as an integrative influence in society (now integrating only the individual). Religious belonging is no longer viewed as a logical outcome of religious belief. Faith no longer inspires strong group loyalties and commitments and is no longer linked to custom, social inheritance, or church going. The "plausibility structures" of religion no longer have a viable social base. Historically and culturally rooted religious symbols become subject to widespread cooptation by both individuals and a variety of secular and religious interest groups. All of these developments reflect the emergence of a Protean form of religion, a highly amorphous "pick and choose" religiosity, one that is reinforced by a market economy ethos that trivializes the experience of grace and the sacred as yet another matter of consumer "taste" and "preference." This situation, as noted earlier, also opens up numerous opportunities for a variety of spiritual gurus and secular therapists to rise to the role of cultural heroes.

Although Campbell was not, himself, of the generational cohort that carried these privatizing shifts and values in religious orientation into the 1980s, his vision of mythology strikes me as entirely congruent with them. As previously noted, Campbell's conceptualization of the hero/savior myth reinforces the idea that the pursuit of a free, gratified, and unalienated "self" is not only desirable, but essential to personal and *spiritual* fulfillment. Campbell's vision of spiritual enlightenment presumes an autonomous individual, one who is on a spiritual "journey," on his or her own "quest," and with little necessary involvement with or connection to a particular religious community. Questions of authority, of discipline, of the common life, of social/ethical consequences, and of the whole system of community representations historically associated with religion have little apparent relevancy to this cause.[82] The first cause is "living out of one's own center" and fulfilling one's own "destiny."[83] Thus, Campbell's "power of myth" both expresses and reinforces the contemporary cultural shift in the direction of a less socially restrained, more privatized, personally expressive, and subjective mode of religiosity. In this regard Campbell's thought belongs in a larger body of cultural reflection that has helped both to de-institutionalize religion and to reduce its external and institutional elements to a purely instrumental role.[84] As such, Campbell's vision of the "power of myth" represents another step in the emancipation of believers from "the tutelage of organized religious collectivities."[85]

Narrative Theology and the Ecological Movement

Other factors that are also relevant to the "Joseph Campbell phenomenon" include the emerging ecology movement and the popularity in recent years of "narrative theology," a perspective that reflects the greater awareness and self-consciousness about religious symbols and mythopoetic views of humanity.

With regard to the ecology movement, Campbell spoke and wrote in terms of an ecological vision that unequivocally repudiated the nature/supernatural dualism and distrust of nature and creation that characterized so much of western religious thought.[86] He called for the need to get back into accord "with the wisdom of nature and realize again our brotherhood with the animals and with the water and the sea."[87] Campbell's thinking in this regard is clearly in line with the emerging ecological movement and, even more significantly, with the philosophical monism that underlies much of it.

With regard to narrative theology, Campbell became popular at a time when, after decades of rationalistic de-emphasis on myth

and symbol in Christianity, "narrative theologians" began redis-
covering the importance of myth and symbols in the search for
meaning and self-understanding. Where the more scientifically
oriented Pierre Teilhard de Chardin had looked to evolution for
evidence of divine power and spiritual development, a contemporary theologian such as John Dunne looks for this in Scriptures,
epics, myths, and stories as do Andrew Greeley,[88] Harvey Cox,[89]
and others.[90] (As Wuthnow has noted, this development indicates
the degree to which theological reflection [and mythology] con-
verges with some aspects of the social sciences in its concern for the
symbolically constructed character of reality.[91])

Not unrelated to the popularity of narrative theology,
Campbell's appeal should also be viewed in the context of the
heightened awareness of the importance of multi-cultural experience. We are now entering another era of tribalism, of heightened
racial and ethnic tensions, separatism and fragmentation and
struggle over the question of a common culture. Campbell's thought
on mythology addresses this issue because it offers an introduction to multi-cultural experience.[92] However, it should be noted
that Campbell's thought also runs contrary to tribalism because
the "power of myth" ultimately emphasizes the importance of our
common humanity, not our personal or social genealogy.

The Media

Finally, it goes without saying that one cannot situate the
significance of the contemporary "Joseph Campbell phenomenon" without considering the role of the mass media. Articles by
and about Campbell and interviews with him began appearing in
popular print (*Time, Psychology Today, Esquire, Parabola*) in the early
1970s and increased in frequency throughout the 1980s. As I noted
at the beginning, Campbell's appearances with Bill Moyers were
his first real exposure to the mass American public, producing an
effect akin to what the Beatles accomplished for Maharishi Mahesh
Yogi and Transcendental Meditation: widespread public visibility
and quasi-celebrity status.

In the Moyers' interviews, Campbell's neighborly and ani-
mated cadence, his encyclopedic-like knowledge, and his engaging manner as the senior statesman of myth struck a very respon-

sive cord, and perhaps especially so in our age-segregated society little accustomed to media exposure to a lively and erudite octogenarian. The Moyer's interviews also highlighted Campbell's mesmerizing skill as a story-teller, another relevant factor in explaining Campbell's appeal. Nor should the fact be overlooked that the "Joseph Campbell phenomenon" continues to be promoted through aggressive marketing and carefully packaged media promotion of his many books and tapes on mythology.

* * * * * *

The popularity of Joseph Campbell and his contribution to contemporary spirituality and the rehabilitation of myth must be situated within the broader realignment of religion and culture in American society that has occurred over the last three decades. This realignment was, itself, the product of complex post-World War II structural changes relating to birth rates, expanded education opportunities, new mobility, and other social, political, and economic changes. Campbell's popular appeal, like that of other new religious seers and pundits of the 1960s, the 1970s, and the 1980s was also facilitated by the "culture crisis" of the time. Furthermore, his views on the "power of myth" were culturally aligned with the renewed emphasis on religious experience, with the expanding interest in mysticism, and with the growing awareness of the cultural and historical relativity of all religious preferences.

Campbell's thought on the "power of myth" also proved congruent with themes in contemporary (especially cognitive) psychology and with Human Potential initiatives that exemplified the broader cultural embrace of a psychologized religiosity and a therapeutic ethos. Campbell's ideas also recapitulated long-standing elements of the American tradition of romantic individualism and contributed to the promotion of privatized religion and heightened spiritual individualism.

The "Joseph Campbell phenomenon" also illustrates anew how the critique of contemporary religion continues to be raised not only from the outside, but also in the name of the "perennial religiosity" within the core of a religion itself.[93] Campbell was another example of a contemporary whose life-world vision was shaped and informed by religious experience, but not constrained by theological dogma or institutional authority. As a spiritual argonaut, Campbell "passed over" to the perspective of other religions. In so doing, he developed deeper insights into the western tradition. However, although the deep structure of his thought and language remained in many ways profoundly Catholic, he remained both an outsider to that tradition and a strident critic of many of its dogmatic and disciplinary aspects. Campbell's "power of myth," in fact, represents a true transvaluation of religion: the use of religious symbolism to attack and critique religious institutions, thereby creating new religious possibilities.

We are, of course, historically too close to know the full extent of the "Joseph Campbell phenomenon" or to make a comprehensive assessment of Campbell's contribution to contemporary American cultural and spiritual life. For those who remain within the Christian tradition, the assessment of Campbell's thought must not avoid the hard questions: Does his "power of myth" represent a new form of Gnosticism and/or Pelagianism? Is it a naive romanticism, or a new and more subtle version of the spiritual will-to-power? Or, is Campbell's thought a harbinger of an emerging spirituality of the future, a spirituality of world-affirmation and of creation that discovers a transcendent dimension in a fundamental engagement in the world and in a human community at once totally autonomous and totally dependent? Does Campbell offer us an authentic call to the transcultural unity which is the basis of all spiritual life and which is absolutely essential to the solution of the ecological crisis the planet now faces? Or, does Campbell's version of the "power of myth" mean a retreat from the burden of history and morality? How does this vision contribute to the well-being of society and synchronize societal requirements with the goals and aspirations of the individual? Does it discriminate between socially valuable desires and socially destructive ones? Is it more than ersatz religiosity or another effort to rescue modern America's "minimal self"? Can we ever "follow our bliss" without some kind of communion and community?

What I have tried to illustrate in this essay is the importance of situating the "Joseph Campbell phenomenon" within the contemporary cultural and historical situation, whatever be the eter-

nal verities of the "power of myth" or whatever may be said about
the character of Campbell's own unconventional life style vis-à-
vis bourgeoisie American society. To situate an individual in a
larger cultural context in no way diminishes the significance of
their contribution. Who of us, after all, stands outside their own
cultural situation?

NOTES

1. This paper approaches Campbell's appeal from a sociology of
knowledge perspective. See Karl Mannheim, *Ideology and Utopia* (New
York: Hartcourt, Brace and Co., 1940).

2. Belden C. Lane, "The Power of Myth: Lessons from Joseph
Campbell," *The Christian Century* (July 5-12, 1989) 652.

3. See "Joseph Campbell: An Exchange," *New York Review of Books*
(November 9, 1989) 57.

4. *Newsweek* (November 14, 1988) 60

5. Campbell noted in an interview that he and Eliade "started in the
same place back to back; I facing the popular community, he the scholarly."
In D.J. Bruckner, "Joseph Campbell: 70 Years of Making Connections,"
New York Times Book Review (December 18, 1983) 28.

6. Joseph Campbell, *The Hero with a Thousand Faces* (New York:
Princeton University Press, 1949) 257.

7. Between 1958 and 1971 Campbell has delivered a series of twenty-
five public talks on mythology in the Great Hall of the Cooper Union
Forum in New York City. These are published in *Myths to Live By* (New
York: Viking Press, 1972). He also began giving talks at the Easlen
Institute in California in 1967.

8. Big Sur Tapes in Tiburon, California, has one of the largest archives
of Campbell lectures recorded over the last twenty years at the Easlen
Institute. Other audio and video tapes of Campbell are commercially
available.

9. See, for example, Robert A. Segal, *Joseph Campbell: An Introduction*
(New York: Garland Publishing Co., 1987). For a less polemic critique of
Campbell, see Florence Sandler and Darrelkl Reeck, "The Masks of
Joseph Campbell," *Religion* 11 (1981) 1-20. For a critique of Campbell's
cultural parochialism, sexism, and for occasional factual errors in his
theory of myth, see Mary R. Lefkowitz, "The Myth of Joseph Campbell,"
The American Scholar 59 (Summer 1990) 429-434.

10. Robert A. Segal, "The Romantic Appeal of Joseph Campbell," *The
Christian Century* 107 (April 4, 1990) 334.

11. For a discussion of these trends, see Sydney E. Ahlstrom, "The
Radical Turn in Theology and Ethics: Why It Occurred in the 1960's," *The*

Annals of the American Academy of Political and Social Science 387 (January 1970) 1-13.

12. See Robert Bellah, *The Broken Covenant: American Civil Religion in a Time of Trial* (New York: Seabury, 1975).

13. Robert Bellah and Charles Glock, eds., *The New Religious Consciousness* (Berkeley: University of California Press, 1976).

14. Robert Bellah, "Religion and Legitimation in the American Republic," in *In Gods We Trust,* eds., Thomas Robbins and Dick Anthony (New Brunswick: Transaction, 1981) 48.

15. The Disciples of Christ, Episcopal, United Church of Christ, United Methodist, and Lutheran Church had by the end of 1987 lost a total of 5.2 million members. See Erling Jordstad, *Holding Fast/Pressing On: Religion in America in the 1980's* (New York: Praeger, 1990) 15.

16. See, for example, Carl S. Dudley, *Where Have All Our People Gone?* (New York: Pilgrim Press, 1979); J. Russell Hale, *The Unchurched: Who Are They and Why They Stay Away* (San Francisco: Harper and Row, 1980); Dean R. Hoge and David A. Roozen, eds., *Understanding Church Growth and Decline* (New York: Pilgrim Press, 1979); Dean M. Kelley, *Why Conservative Churches Are Growing* (San Francisco: Harper and Row, 1972; rev. ed., 1977; rev. ed. Macon, GA: Mercer University Press, 1986); *The Unchurched American* (Princeton: The Princeton Religion Research Center, 1978); Wade Clark Roof, "America's Voluntary Establishment: Mainline Religion in Transition," *Daedalus* 111,1 (Winter 1982) 165-184.

17. See Steven M. Tipton, *Getting Saved from the Sixties* (Berkeley: University of California Press, 1982).

18. See Richard John Neuhaus, *The Naked Public Square* (Grand Rapids: William B. Eerdmans Publishing Co., 1984).

19. For example, see Campbell's remarks throughout *Myths to Live by;* see also Campbell's essay "Mythological Themes in Creative Art and Literature," in *Myths, Dreams and Religion,* ed., Joseph Campbell (Dallas: Spring Publication, Inc., 1988) 138-175.

20. See Jorling, *Holding Fast/Pressing On* and Ronald B. Flowers, *Religion in Strange Times: The 1960's and 1970's* (Macon, GA: Mercer University Press, 1984).

21. See Langdon Gilkey, *Society and the Sacred: Toward a Theology of Culture in Decline* (New York: Crossroads, 1981); Gabriel A. Almond, Marvin Chodorow, and Roy Harvey Pearce, *Progress and Its Discontents* (Berkeley: University of California Press, 1982); and Peter Berger, "From the Crisis of Religion to the Crisis of Secularity," in *Religion in America: Spirituality in a Secular Age,* eds., Mary Douglas and Steven M. Tipton (Boston: Beacon Press, 1982) 14-24.

22. See Robert Wuthnow, *The Restructuring of American Religion* (Princeton: Princeton University Press), esp. chapter 7.

23. For a useful compendium of findings from national samples of survey data from Gallup's American Institute of Public Opinion, the National Opinion Research Center's semi-annual General Social Survey, and the Survey Research Center of the University of Michigan confirming this point, see Andrew M. Greeley, *Religious Change in America* (Boston: Harvard University Press, 1989). See also Wade Clark Roof and William McKinney, *American Mainline Religion: Its Changing Shape and Future* (New Brunswick: Rutgers University Press, 1988) and Robert Wuthnow, *The Restructuring of American Religion.* As Greeley has noted, the slight rise in those who describe themselves as non-religious is due to the baby-boom demographic bulge (a function of age) rather than an increase in secularizing tendencies in American society; see Greeley, *Religious Change.*

24. See, for example, Ronald B. Flowers, *Religion in Strange Times: The 1960's and 1970's* (Macon, GA: Mercer University Press, 1984); Jorstad, *Holding Fast/Pressing On*; Daniel Bell, "Religion in the Sixties," *Social Research* 38 (Autumn 1971) 447-497; James M. Gustafson, ed., "The Sixties: Radical Change in American Religion," *The Annals of the American Academy of Political and Social Science* 387 (January 1970). For a popular account of these developments by the early seventies, see "searching Again for the Sacred," *Time* (April 9, 1973) 90-93. See also the special edition "Religion in America Today," *The Annals of the American Academy of Political and Social Science* 480 (July 1985).

25. See William G. McGouglin, *Revivals, Awakenings, and Reform* (Chicago: University of Chicago Press, 1978); Tom Wolf, "The Me Decade and the Third Great Awakening," *New West* (August 30, 1976) 27-48.

26. See Wade Clark Roof and William McKinney, "Denominational America and the New Religious Pluralism," *The Annals of the American Academy of Political and Social Science* 480 (July 1985) 28.

27. As Wuthnow notes, these varying strategies and adaptations by the religious right and left were, themselves, a consequence of the widening "education gap" in social attitudes and religion that became evident by the 1970s and even more pronounced during the next decade. See Wuthnow, *The Restructuring of American Religion* 168.

28. See Joseph Campbell, "The Secularization of the Sacred," in *The Religious Situation*, ed., Donald R. Culter, vol. 1 (Boston: Beacon Press, 1968) 601-637.

29. On this point, see Sandler and Reeck, "The Masks" 1-2.

30. For an insightful chronicle of this latter phenomenon, see Jay Stevens, *Storming Heaven: LSD and the American Dream* (New York: Atlantic Monthly Press, 1987).

31. Winston King, "Eastern Religions: A New Interest and Influence," *The Annals* 387 (January 1970) 66-76. The "new religious consciousness"

also had distinctive class characteristics, centering in large part around affluent "baby boomers" whose prolonged adolescence and greater discretionary time allowed for widespread cultural experimentation. See Robert Wuthnow, *The Conscious Reformation* (Berkeley and Los Angeles: University of California Press, 1976); and *Experimentation in American Religion* (Berkeley and Los Angeles: University of California Press, 1978).

32. Theodore Roszak, *The Making of a Counter Culture* (Garden City, NY: Doubleday, 1969); also Charles Reich, *The Greening of America* (New York: Random House, 1970).

33. See Campbell, *The Mythic Image.*

34. Campbell, *Myths to Live By* 96-97.

35. *Newsweek* (November 14, 1988) 61; also Campbell, "Mythical Themes in Creative Literature and Art" 148; Joseph Campbell, *The Power of Myth,* with Bill Moyers (New York: Doubleday, 1988) 60.

36. Joseph Campbell, *The Masks of God: Creative Mythology* (New York: Penguin Books, 1976) 7.

37. Lane, "The Power of Myth" 653.

38. In Cutler, ed., *The Religious Situation* 601-637.

39. See Stevens, *Storming Heaven.*

40. McLoughlin points out that this interest and its experiential orientation had been prefigured by theologians such as Thomas Altizer and Gabriel Vahanian who asserted that the "death of God" marked the passage from transcendence to immanence, but not the immanence of theistic evolutionists, but an antinomian immanence where God's power is available through the heart, not the intellect. See *Revivals, Awakenings, and Reform* 193.

41. This development was captured in Tom Wolfe's classic satire, "The Me Decade."

42. See for instance the published studies based on the San Francisco Survey Project in the early 1970s. Charles Y. Glock and Robert N. Bellah, eds., *The New Religious Consciousness* (Berkeley and Lost Angeles: University of California Press, 1976); Robert Wuthnow, *The Consciousness Reformation* (Berkeley and Los Angeles: The University of California Press, 1976); and *Experimentation in American Religion: The New Mysticisms and Their Implications for the Churches* (Berkeley and Los Angeles: University of California Press, 1978). See also Andrew Greeley, *Ecstasy: A Way of Knowing* (Englewood Cliffs, NJ: Prentice-Hall, 1974).

43. Campbell, *Myths to Live By* 244.

44. Joseph Campbell, *The Hero with a Thousand Faces* (Princeton: Princeton University Press, 1968) 391.

45. Segal, "The Romantic Appeal" 334.

46. Campbell's remark in *Time* (January 17, 1972) 51.

47. Eugene Kennedy, "Earthrise" The Dawning of a New Spiritual Awareness," *New York Times Magazine* (April 15, 1979) 14-15; see also Campbell's remarks in *Myths, Dreams, and Religion* 145.

48. Campbell, *Creative Mythology* 32.

49. Joseph Campbell, *The Masks of God: Creative Mythology* (New York: Penguin books, 1968) 671.

50. Ibid. 637.

51. See Philip Rieff, *The Triumph of the Therapeutic* (Chicago: University of Chicago Press, 1987) 128; also Paul C. Vitz, *Psychology as Religion: The Cult of Self Worship* (Grand Rapids: William B. Eerdmans, 1979).

52. Ibid. 199.

53. See Wuthnow, *The Restructuring of American Religion* 300-301.

54. Campbell asserted that in exposing his students to the commonality of myth, their Christian and Jewish symbols would be reinforced because "they now had psychological value to them." In John M. Maher and Dennie Briggs, *An Open Life: Joseph Campbell in Conversation with Michael Toms* (New York: Harper and Row, 1989) 61.

55. Rieff, *The Triumph of the Therapeutic* 114. Rieff's critique of Jung (esp. chapter 5 in particular) has similar applicability to Campbell's religio-mythology.

56. Maher and Briggs, *An Open Life* 62.

57. For a survey of Americans who have become seekers of self-fulfillment and preoccupied with inner psychological needs, see Daniel Yankelovich, "New Rules in American Life," *Psychology Today* (April 1981).

58. See Jorstad, *Holding Fast/Passing On* 151-184.

59. The work of Carl Rogers, Abraham Maslow, Rollo May, Viktor Frankl, Roberto Assagioli, and Stanislav Grof is relevant here. For a more contemporary expression, see also Mihaly Csikszentmihalyi, *Flow: The Psychology of Optimal Experience* (New York: Harper and Row, 1990). Campbell's psychological interpretation of myth also paralleled Bettleheim's heavily (and equally popular) psychological interpretation of fairy tales which also gained popularity in the 1970s. See Bruno Bettelheim, *The Uses of Enchantment* (New York: Alfred A. Knopf, 1976).

60. Yankelovich, "New Rules in American Life" 1989.

61. Campbell, *The Power of Myth* 124.

62. Campbell, *The Hero* 388.

63. Sandler and Reeck, "The Masks" 14.

64. Campbell, *Creative Mythology* 41.

65. See especially Campbell's discussion of "Experience and Authority" in *Creative Mythology* 3-42.

66. See Campbell, *The Power of Myth* 155.

67. See, for example, the discussion by Dick Francis and Thomas Robbins in "Spiritual Innovation and the Crisis of American Civil Religion," in *Religion and America: Spirituality in a Secular Age*, eds., Douglas and Tipton, 229-249. See also the comments by Roberta H. Markman and Robert Markman that much of the fascination with Campbell's ideas stemmed from "the recurrent disillusionment with politics"; in the *New York Review of Books* (November 9, 1989) 59. Already in *The Hero* Campbell also makes the point that social problems stem essentially from "psychological ones" (121). This is a basic theme that appears again in "New Age" ideology; see editorial in *The 1989 Guide to New Age Living* (P.O. Box 853, Farmingdale, NY, 1988) 103.

68. Campbell, *The Power of Myth* 65-66.

69. Ibid. 161.

70. Wolfe, "The Me Decade" 48.

71. Yankelovich, "New Rules in American Life" 1981.

72. See Brendan Gill, "The Faces of Joseph Campbell," *The New York Review of Books* (September 28, 1989) 16-18-19. Responses to Gill's article were published in the November 9, 1989 (57) issue.

73. See *The New York Review* (November 9, 1989) 58.

74. On this point, see K.C. Cole, "Master of the Myth," *Newsweek* (November 14, 1988) 63.

75. Campbell, *The Power of Myth* 99.

76. John F. Wilson, "The Sociological Study of American Religion," in Charles H. Lippy and Peter N. Williams, eds., *Encyclopedia of American Religious Experience*, vol. 1 (New York: Scribner, 1988) 28.

77. See, for example, Bryan R. Wilson, *Contemporary Transformations of Religion* (Oxford: Oxford University Press, 1972).

78. For discussion of this issue, see Robert N. Bellah and others, *Habits of the Heart* (Berkeley: University of California Press, 1985); Wade C. Roof and William McKinney, *American Mainline Religion: Its Changing Shape and Future* (New Brunswick: Rutgers University Press, 1987); Thomas Luckmann, *The Invisible Religion* (London: Macmillan, 1967); Christopher Lasch, *The Culture of Narcissism* (New York: Norton, 1978). See also *The "Unchurched American"_Study* (Gallup Organization, Inc., 1978) and Jorstad, *Holding Fast/Pressing On* esp 129-167.

79. One of the classic canons in this regard is Emerson's essay "On Self-Reliance" in which he extolled Americans to trust the "aboriginal Self on which a universal reliance may be grounded," admonished them that "Whoso would be a man, must be a nonconformist," and held that "to believe that what is true for you in our private heart is true for all

men—that is genius." In Robert H. Hossum and John K. Roth, *American Ground, Vistas, Visions, & Revisions: A Reader in American Studies* (New York: Paragon House, 1988) 164-167.

80. Jorstad, *Holding Fast/Pressing On* 129.

81. Luckmann, *The Invisible Religion*

82. This point is made by Clark and McKinney in reference to the wider cultural trends in this direction in *American Mainline Religion* 41.

83. Campbell, *Myths to Live By* 68. See also Campbell's assertion that "Pelagianism today is the only brand of Christianity with any possibility of an Occidental future." In Campbell, "The Secularization of the Sacred," in Cutler, ed., *The Religious Situation* 614.

84. See Louis Dupré, "Spiritual Life in a Secular Age," in Douglas and Tipton, eds., *Religion and America* 3-14.

85. Roof and McKinney, *American Mainline Religion* 44.

86. See, for example, Campbell, *The Power of Myth* 98-99; *Creative Mythology* 20-22.

87. Campbell, *The Power of Myth* 31.

88. Andrew Greeley, *Unsecular Man: The Persistence of Religion* (New York: Schocken, 1972).

89. Harvey Cox, *The Feast of Fools* (Cambridge: Harvard University Press, 1969).

90. See, for example, Peter Berger's *A Rumor of Angels* (Garden City: Doubleday, 1969).

91. Wuthnow, *The Restructuring of American Religion* 298; also Robert Bellah, "Christianity and Symbolic Realism," *Journal for the Scientific Study of Religion* 9 (Summer 1970) 89-96.

92. A point made by Lefkowitz in "The Myth of Joseph Campbell" 434.

93. See Michael Fuss, "New Age and Europe: A Challenge for Theology," in FIUC *Research Project on New Religious Movements* (Rome: Dossier, 1990) 873.

CHAPTER THREE

Joseph Campbell's Antithesis: Myth Versus Religion

Robert Segal

"My favorite definition of religion, declares Joseph Campbell, "is 'a misinterpretation of mythology'" (*Open* 78-79). No theorist of myth since the Victorian Indologist F. Max Müller pits myth against religion as severely as Campbell does. Typically, theorists view myth either as tied to religion or at least as compatible with religion. The antithesis that Campbell draws between myth and religion is the subject of this chapter.

What the actual relationship is between myth and religion depends first on the definition of both phenomena. Most theorists assume a conventional definition of religion: the belief in one or more gods. It is over the definition of myth that there is dispute. When myth is defined as a story about one or more gods, the relationship between myth and religion is obviously intimate. But when myth is defined as, say, an important story of any kind, the agents can be humans or even animals. In hero myths the subjects are more often human than divine.

Myth need not even be defined as a story. It can refer to a sheer conviction like the American myths of the frontier and of the self-made man. Some mythic convictions do involve gods. For example, the myths of America as Eden and as the possessor of a manifest destiny presuppose God's scrutiny. But other myths, including those of the frontier and of the self-made man, involve no gods. In short, myth need not be defined in religious terms.

41

Myth and Religion for Theorists of Myth

The relationship between myth and religion depends not only on the definition of myth but also on the theory of myth. For anthropologists Edward Tylor[1] and James Frazer,[2] myth falls wholly within religion. Religion for them arises to explain and control the physical world, and myth is an aspect of the religious explanation. Religion *sans* myth provides the names, relationships, and attributes of the gods; myth provides stories that illustrate or explain those characteristics. The classicist Jane Harrison[3] and the biblicist S.H. Hooke[4] link myth to religious ritual, for which myth provides the script.

For all four, myth ascribes the nature of the world to the recurrent actions of gods exclusively. For anthropologist Bronislaw Malinowski[5] and historian of religions Mircea Eliade,[6] myth ascribes the nature of the world to the past actions of either gods or humans. The world is as it is today—for example, the ground must be tilled to yield food—because of what either gods or humans did long ago. Insofar as the agents in myth can be humans, myth for Malinowski and Eliade is not necessarily tied to religion. Yet insofar as earliest humans had the power to set the course of the world forever, they are akin to gods. For Eliade, myth not only explains what happened long ago but actually transports one back to that pristine time and thereby brings one closer to the god or god-like figures, who were nearer then than they are now.

Both Sigmund Freud[7] and Carl Jung[8] allow for myths with other than a divine subject. Freud and Jung connect myths most tightly to dreams, not religion. The chief myths for Freudians are hero myths, in which the subjects are usually human, not divine.[9] For Jung, there are archetypes of natural phenomena, human roles, artifacts, abstractions, and events as well as of gods. For Jungians and perhaps Freudians, religion is always tied to myth, but myth is not always tied to religion. Indeed, Jungian patients are commonly lapsed believers seeking a "post-religious" meaning. Finally, for Freud and Jung the true, unconscious meaning of myth has nothing to do with the external world and so with the gods. It deals instead with the human mind.

Campbell's Interpretation of Religious Myth

Campbell's position on the relationship of myth to religion gets more doctrinaire as he gets older. Originally for him the two work in sync. In his early commentary on the Grimms' fairy tales (1943) he outright defines myths as "religious recitations conceived as symbolic of the play of Eternity in Time."[10] More typically, he allows for secular as well as religious myths. In *The Hero with a Thousand Faces* (1949) he interposes secular with religious myths. In the first three volumes of *The Masks of God* (1959-1964) all of the myths discussed are religious—not, however, because Campbell is excluding secular myths but simply because the mythologies discussed are religious ones.

Only in volume three of *Masks, Occidental Mythology* does the division between myth and religion begin to surface. Here the distinction is not yet between myth and religion but merely between myth rightly interpreted and myth misinterpreted by religion, and misinterpreted only by western religion. Campbell asserts that mainstream Judaism, Christianity, Islam, together with ancient Greek and Roman religions, systematically misconstrue their own myths. While he grants correct interpretations by marginal, heterodox movements like Gnosticism, he argues that in the west conventional believers have systematically been inculcated in a false understanding of myth.

According to Campbell, western religions uniformly interpret their myths literally, historically, and particularistically: as descriptions of past, one-time events in the lives of native gods and countrymen. Furthermore, western religions uniformly interpret their myths nonmystically and patriarchally: as descriptions, not to say endorsements, of an unbridgeable divide at once between humans and gods and between females and males. Gods rule over humans, and males rule over females— both in heaven and on earth.

Campbell assumes that the sole correct interpretation of all myths is symbolic, ahistorical, universalistic, mystical, and matriarchal. Both the east and primitive peoples correctly decipher their own myths. Only the west misconstrues its myths.

To take an example, Campbell assumes that mainstream Judaism and Christianity regularly take chapter three of Genesis to be saying that once upon a time a primordial couple resided in a garden called Eden. For Campbell, Eden in fact symbolizes the unconscious, the original portion of the mind from which consciousness arose: "The Garden of Eden is a metaphor for that innocence that is innocent of time, innocent of opposites, and that is the prime center out of which consciousness then becomes aware of the changes" (*Power* 50). Eden symbolizes not a place but a state of mind. Departure from Eden symbolizes not a past event but a recurrent one, an event in the lives not just of our forebears but of all humans: the emergence of consciousness out of the unconscious.

For Campbell, the symbolic meaning of every myth is not only psychological but also metaphysical: "Hence, the figurations of myth are metaphorical . . . in *two* senses simultaneously, as bearing (1) *psychological*, but at the same time (2) *metaphysical*, connotations" (*Inner* 56). Just as every myth discloses the existence of an unconscious as well as a conscious mind, so every one discloses the existence of an invisible as well as a visible cosmos:

> And so, to grasp the full value of the mythological figures that have come down to us, we must understand that they are not only symptoms of the unconscious (as indeed are all human thoughts and acts) but also controlled and intended statements of certain spiritual principles . . . Briefly formulated, the universal doctrine teaches that all the visible structures of the world-all things and beings—are the effects of a ubiquitous power out of which they rise, which supports and fills them during the period of their manifestation, and back into which they must ultimately dissolve (*Hero* 257).

If psychologically Eden symbolizes the unconscious, metaphysically it symbolizes immaterial, ultimate reality. Metaphysically, departure from Eden symbolizes the development of the created, material world out of the pre-existent one.

Campbell assumes that mainstream Judaism and Christianity also interpret chapter three of Genesis as saying that God should rule over humans and males over females. Hence Adam and Eve get punished for seeking to become gods, and Eve's punishment is subordination to Adam. For Campbell, the myth actually advocates the opposite: it advocates both mysticism and matriarchy. Where hierarchy is for Campbell a male quality, equality, which for him means outright identity, is a female one. Matriarchy thus means the dissolution of the very distinction between male and female rather than, as one might expect, female dominance, which for him would be merely the flip side of male hierarchy. Campbell associates matriarchy with mysticism, which involves the dissolution of all other distinctions as well:

> The patriarchal point of view is distinguished from the earlier archaic [i.e., matriarchal] view by its setting apart of all pairs-of-opposites—male and female, life and death, true and false, good and evil—as though they were absolutes in themselves and not merely aspects of the larger entity of life. This we may liken to a solar, as opposed to lunar, mythic view, since darkness flees from the sun as its opposite, but in the moon dark and light interact in the one sphere (*Occidental* 26-27).

Psychologically, the Garden of Eden story says not only that there exists an unconscious as well as a conscious mind but also that those two minds are really one. Metaphysically, the story says not only that there exists an immaterial as well as a material one but also that those two worlds are actually one. The story says as well that divinity and humanity are one and that females and males are one.

The mysticism that, according to Campbell, all myths express is of a world-affirming rather than world-rejecting variety. Rather than declaring that everything is immaterial rather than material, divine rather than human, or female rather than male, myth espouses the identity of immateriality with matter, of gods with humans, and of females with males, Just as Campbell's hero returns to the everyday world to find within it the new world he thought he had left behind, so all who imbibe the message of myth find the new world within, not beyond, the everyday one. Indeed, the new world does not just lie *within* the everyday world but *is* the everyday world. The two worlds are mystically one.[11]

Campbell equates Eve with a female god and contends that her rebellion against God represents an attempt by defeated female gods to regain power. The male serpent and Adam are somehow on the female side. In keeping the trio from becoming gods themselves, God quells the rebellion and thereby preserves patriarchy:

> Thus Yahweh cursed the woman to bring forth in pain and be subject to her spouse—which set the seal of the patriarchy on the new age. And he cursed, also, the man who had come to the tree and eaten of the fruit that she presented (*Occidental* 29).

But Campbell then maintains that the earth to which Adam and Eve will, as dust, one day be returning symbolizes the mother goddess, who in receiving back her children ultimately triumphs over God. Campbell even suggests that at death Adam and Eve will again become one, as Eve was before emerging from Adam's rib. The reunion of male with female is, again, an expression of victorious matriarchy:

> But the ground, the dust, out of which the punished couple had been taken, was, of course, the goddess Earth, deprived of her anthropomorphic features, yet retaining in her elemental aspect her function of furnishing the substance into which the new spouse, Yahweh, had breathed the breath of her children's life. And they were to return to her, not to the father, in death. Our of her they had been taken, and to her they would return . . . Adam and Eve were thus the children of the mother-goddess Earth. They had been one at first, as Adam; then split in two, as Adam and Eve . . . "The man," we read, "called his wife's name Eve, because she was the mother of all living."
>
> As the mother of all living, Eve herself, then, must be recognized as the missing anthropomorphic aspect of the mother-goddess. And Adam, therefore, must have been her son as well as spouse: for the legend of the rib is clearly a patriarchal inversion (giving precedence to the male) of the earlier myth of the hero born from the goddess Earth [i.e., Eve], who returns to her to be reborn (*Occidental* 29-30).

Even if Adam returns to the mother goddess Earth in order to be reborn, his return to her and his rebirth out of her evince his divine roots.

Campbell does not deny that on the surface chapter three of Genesis is interpretable historically, nonmystically, and patriarchally (e.g., *Occidental* 114). He simply denies that this interpretation is correct. He claims not merely that there is an additional way of interpreting the Bible but that there is only one correct way. He argues that the Bible does not merely echo a dead matriarchal, mystical religion but still bespeaks that religion.

> . . . the mythic imagery of the Bible bears a message of its own that may not always be the one verbalized in the discourse of the text . . . [I]n the context of the patriarchy of the Iron Age Hebrews of the first millennium B.C., the [matriarchal] mythology adopted from the earlier neolithic and Bronze Age civilizations of the lands they occupied and for a time ruled became inverted . . . [T]here is consequently an ambivalence inherent in many of the basic symbols of the Bible that no amount of rhetorical stress on the patriarchal interpretation can suppress. They address a pictorial message to the heart that exactly reverses the verbal message addressed to the brain; and this nervous discord inhabits both Christianity and Islam as well as Judaism, since they too share in the legacy of the Old Testament (*Occidental* 110, 17).

Properly understood, according to Campbell, the Bible speaks not historically but mythically:

> The world is full of origin myths, and all are factually [i.e., historically] false. The world is full, also, of great traditional books tracing the history of man . . . On the surface they may appear to have been composed as conscientious history. In depth they reveal themselves to have been conceived as myths: poetic readings of the mystery of life from a certain interested point of view. But to read a poem as a chronicle of fact is—to say the least—to miss the point (*Occidental* 95).

According to Campbell, the Bible, properly deciphered, bears the same message as eastern and primitive mythologies: "No one familiar with the mythologies of the goddess of the primitive, ancient, and oriental worlds can turn to the Bible without recognizing counterparts on every page, transformed, however, to render an argument contrary to the older faiths" (*Occidental* 9). That common message is of the mystical oneness between humans and god:

> The orthodox Christian notion that nature is corrupt and the Christian Church incorruptible can be said to represent an extreme statement of the implications of the Jewish myth of God apart from the world . . . Ironically, however, the very symbols used by the Church to teach of this supposed circumstances bore in themselves implicitly a contrary instruction . . . The little image of Mary . . . tells first, that, as Eckhart knew, the Trinity is immanent in each of us and to be born by us in our knowledge; second, that, as the Cretans knew, the goddess is the mother womb, the ultimate bound of all existence; and third, as all the world seems to have known except our own authorized interpreters of the icons of our common heritage: microcosm and macrocosm are in essence one in God—who is by no means corrupt, corruptible, or to be mocked by any definition of creed (*Occidental* 516-517).

Campbell's Advocacy of Secular Myth

In *Masks: Occidental* Campbell is making a double claim: first, that the Bible has invariably been taken literally by conventional Judaism and Christianity, and, second, that it has thereby been perverted. Yet these claims pale beside the third, bolder one that initially emerges in *Creative Mythology* (1968), the fourth and final volume of *Masks*: the claim that myth is to be severed from religion per se. In *Masks: Occidental* Campbell argues boldly that western religions misunderstand their own myths. In *Masks: Creative* he argues even more boldly that the true meaning of myth is secular. Where in *Masks: Occidental* religious myths, correctly grasped, preach oneness between humans and god, in *Masks: Creative* religious myths, correctly grasped, are not even referring to god. In *Masks: Occidental* Campbell daringly contrasts the inevitable misinterpretation of myths by westerners to the unfailingly correct interpretation of them by easterners and primitives. In *Masks: Creative* he much more daringly dismisses even eastern and primitive religions, not just western ones, for interpreting myths as referring to god.

By "creative" mythology Campbell means modern western mythology, which for him dates all the way back to the twelfth century. The pioneering creative myths are Gottfried von Strassburg's *Tristan* and Wolfram von Eschenbach's *Parzival*. Both espouse world-affirming rather than world-rejecting mysticism. In the first three volumes of *Masks* Campbell praises the east precisely for its world-affirming mysticism and damns the west for its world-rejecting anti-mysticism. Now the east as well as the earlier west gets dismissed for a world-rejecting stance, be it mystical or nonmystical. Creative mythology alone now affirms the everyday world, for it alone is secular. Religion per se now proves otherworldly: union with god now removes one from the everyday world. At the same time Campbell maintains his unrelenting conviction that, despite appearances, all myths harbor the same meaning.[12] More precisely, then, he praises creative mythologists for alone *recognizing* the world-affirming, thereby secular outlook of even "religious" mythologies.

What Campbell says of Wolfram applies to Gottfried was well:

> Moreover, he [Wolfram] applied his interpretations consciously to an altogether *secular* mythology, of men and women living for *this* world, not "that," pursuing earthly, human, and humane (i.e., in Wolfram's terms, "courtly") purposes, and supported in their spiritual tasks not by a supernatural grace dispensed by way of sacraments but by the *natural* grace of individual endowment and the worldly virtue of loyalty in love. That is what gives to his work its epochal significance as the first example in the history of world literature of a *consciously developed secular Christian myth* (*Creative* 476).

Creative mythology frees the individual from submission to god and the group alike, both of which turn one away from the world:

> In Wolfram's *Parzival* the boon is to be the inauguration of a new age of the human spirit: of *secular* spirituality, sustained by self-responsible individuals acting not in terms of general laws supposed to represent the will of some personal god or impersonal eternity, but each in terms of his own developing realization of worth. Such an idea is distinctly—and uniquely—European (*Creative* 480).

By contrast, primitive, eastern, and earlier western mythologies suppress individuality in the name of god and the group:

> And so we may say in summary at this point that the first and absolutely essential characteristic of the new, secular mythology that was emerging in the literature of the twelfth and thirteenth centuries was that its structuring themes were not derived from dogma, learning, politics, or any current concepts of the general social good, but were expressions of individual experience: what I have termed Libido as opposed to Credo. Undoubtedly the myths of all traditions, great and small, must have sprung in the first instance from individual experiences... However, in so far as these then became the authorized and even sanctified vehicles of established cultural heritages, overinterpreted as of divine origin and enforced often on pain of death... they were no longer determined by, but were rather determinants of, individual experience, feeling, thought, and motivation . . . Traditional mythologies, that is to say, whether of the primitive or of the higher cultures, antecede and control experience; whereas what I am here calling Creative Mythology is an effect and expression of experience. Its producers do not claim divine authority for their human, all too human, works (*Creative* 64-65).

In order to distinguish the individualistic, later western outlook from all other ones, Campbell in the essay "The Secularization of the Sacred" (1968) argues that the modern ethos represents the resurfacing of a pagan pre-Christian tradition that Christianity had vainly sought to eradicate. Campbell labels this tradition European and identifies it with one of the strains forming the west: the strain composed of Greeks, Romans, Celts, and Germans (*Flight* 215). The twelfth century marks the beginning of the continuing revolt by this individualistic, European strain against the collectivist, Near Eastern one, which is composed of Jews, Muslims, and above all Christians:

> The great period of the breakthrough of the native European spirit against the imposed authority of decisions made by a lot of Levantine [i.e., Near Eastern] bishops at the Councils of Nicaea, Constantinople, Ephesus, and Chalcedon (fourth to eighth centuries A.D.), occurred in the twelfth and thirteenth centuries . . .

As I see it, this breakthrough followed as the consequence of the courage of an increasing number of people of great stature to credit their own experience and to live by it against the dictates of authority (*Flight* 208).

As exemplars of this anti-Christian revolt, *Tristan* and *Parzival* vaunt worldly, individualistic experience in favor of otherworldly, institutionalized religion.

Though himself probably a cleric, and certainly learned in theology, Gottfried is openly disdainful of current Christian doctrines . . . Chiefly, Gottfried's inspiration had sprung from his recognition in the Celtic legend . . . [of] an order of poetic imagery congenial to his own mode of experience. It was a legend rooted, like all Arthurian romance, in the most ancient native European mythological tradition—that of the old megalithic, bronze-age goddess of many names . . . The Grail legend, also, had sprung from that pagan base . . . [I]n rejecting absolutely the authority of the Church, these lovers and poets returned consciously and conscientiously to an earlier pre-Christian, native European order of conscience, wherein the immanence of divinity was recognized in nature and its productions . . . (*Flight* 216-217, 222).

For Campbell, courtly love epitomizes the world-affirming view of creative mythology. *Eros*, as lust, is sheer worldliness. *Agape*, as selfless love for one's neighbor, is equivalent to otherworldliness. *Amor*, or courtly love, alone combines the two.[13] Rather than the cultivation of either the body (*eros*) or the soul (*agape*), *amor* cultivates the soul in the body. Indeed, it cultivates the soul *as* the body:

For there is no such thing as a love that is either purely spiritual or merely sensual. Man is composed of body and spirit (if we may still use such terms) and is thus an essential mystery in himself; and the deepest heart of this mystery (in Gottfried's view) is the very point touched and wakened by—and in— the mystery of love, the sacramental purity of which has nothing whatsoever to do with a suspension or suppression of the sensuous and the senses, but includes and even rests upon the physical realization (*Creative* 248).

To the ideals of courtly love, voiced by both *Tristan* and *Parzival*, Campbell contrasts the self-sacrificing, hence other worldly values of primitives, the east, and the earlier west:

> ... Wolfram solved the spiritual problem of his century first by setting the ideal of love above marriage and, simultaneously, the ideal of an indissoluble marriage beyond love . . . As far as I know, he was the first poet in the world to put forward seriously this socially explosive ideal of marriage, which has become today, however, the romantic norm of the West, resisted and even despised in the Orient as archaic, immoral, and insane. For through it are transcended the primitive, ancient, and Oriental orders of tribal and family marriage, where social, political, and economic considerations prevail over personal and romantic, and where the unfolding personality . . . is bound back, cropped and trained to the interests of a group (*Creative* 567-568).

For all Campbell's antithesis of secular myth to religion, he does characterize *Parzival* as the first example of a "secular Christian myth" (*Creative* 476), he does say that the native European tradition recognizes the "immanence of divinity" (*Flight* 222), and he does title his essay the "secularization" rather than the elimination of the sacred. He also describes Thomas Mann and James Joyce, his twentieth-century counterparts to Gottfried and Wolfram, as Protestant and Catholic exemplars of the secular impulse (*Creative* 372). It would, then, be going too far to say that Campbell opposes secular myth to true religious experience and even true Christianity.

But it would not be going too far to say that Campbell opposes secular myth to *religion*, by which he means institutionalized religion. Because Campbell lauds creative mythologists for first recognizing the secular nature of all myths, it would not be going too far to say that he opposes myth per se to religion. Certainly in subsequent works he contrasts the two: "Mythology is poetry, and the poetic language is very flexible. Religion turns poetry into prose" (*Power* 141-142).

Campbell's view of the relationship of myth to religion is radical among theorists of myth not because he allows for secular myths but because, from *Masks: Creative* on, he does not allow for religious ones. "Religious myth" comes to be a contradiction in terms. As, again, Campbell states, "My favorite definition of religion is 'a misinterpretation of mythology'" (*Open* 78).

Myth and Science for Campbell

Many of the theorists who join myth to religion pit both against science. By contrast, Campbell not only pits myth against religion but also pits religiously interpreted myth against science. Taken literally, as Campbell assumes ordinary Jews and Christians wrongly take them, biblical myths are undone by science. To cite Campbell's favorite example:

> For example, Jesus ascended to heaven. The denotation would seem to be that somebody ascended to the sky. That's literally what's being said. But if that were really the meaning of the message, then we have to throw it away, because there would have been no such place for Jesus literally to go. We know that Jesus could not have ascended to heaven because there is no physical heaven anywhere in the universe. Even ascending at the speed of light, Jesus would still be in the galaxy. Astronomy and physics have simply eliminated that as a literal, physical possibility (*Power* 56).

Myth severed from religion is fully compatible with science because, taken rightly, it deals with the human mind and with ultimate reality than with the external world. Even the second of Campbell's four standard functions of myth—providing a symbolic image for the world—does not make myth an explanation of the world. Rather, myth provides a metaphor for the world such as that of a Great Chain of Being. Just as "secular Christian" myths began replacing biblical ones back in the twelfth century, so wholly secular non-Christian ones are now replacing any lingering biblical ones. Campbell predicts that contemporary myths, epitomized by the "Star Wars" saga, will take outer space as their backdrop.

Campbell even says that any effective contemporary mythology "must be up-to-date scientifically, based on a concept of the universe that is current, accepted, and convincing" ("Art" 144). For Campbell, the Bible is irretrievable because it is "founded in a cosmological image from the second millennium B.C., which was already out of date when the Bible was put together in the last centuries B.C. and the first A.D. ("Art" 145). Despite Campbell's own enchanting reinterpretation of biblical myths, he despairs of their revival. For him, they are dead and cannot be resurrected. Rather than striving to liberate the Bible from the clutches of its literalist devotees, he abandons it altogether.

Campbell goes so far as to make science itself mythic:

MOYERS: One of the intriguing points of your scholarship is that you do not believe science and mythology conflict.

CAMPBELL: No, they don't conflict. Science is breaking through now into the mystery dimensions. It's pushed itself into the sphere the myth is talking about. It's come to the edge.

MOYERS: The edge being—

CAMPBELL: —the edge, the interface between what can be known and what is never to be discovered because it is a mystery that transcends all human research (*Power* 132).

In the nineteenth century it was fashionable to set myth and religion against science. In the twentieth century it has become fashionable to reconcile myth and religion with science. Campbell is distinctive among twentieth-century theorists in setting religion against science while reconciling myth with science. He is atypical among theorists of either century in setting myth against religion.*

* This chapter is a somewhat revised version of an essay, originally entitled "Myth Versus Religion for Campbell" which appeared in *Joseph Campbell: Uses of Comparative Mythology*, ed., Kenneth L. Golden (New York: Garland Publishing, 1991). It is reprinted with the permission of both Garland Publishing and Kenneth Golden.

NOTES

1.   Edward B. Tylor, *Primitive Culture*, 2 vols., 1st ed. (London: Murray, 1871).

2.   James G. Frazer, *The Golden Bough*, 12 vols., 3d ed. (London: Macmillan, 1911-1915).

3.   Jane Harrison, *Prolegomena to the Study of Greek Religion* (Cambridge: Cambridge University Press, 1903).

4.   S.H. Hooke, "The Myth and Ritual Pattern of the Ancient East," in *Myth and Ritual,* ed., S.H. Hooke (London: Oxford University Press, 1933)1-14.

5.   Bronislaw Malinowski, *Myth in Primitive Psychology* (London: Routledge and Kegan Paul; New York, Norton, 1926).

6.   Mircea Eliade, *Myth and Reality,* trans., Willard R. Trask (New York: Harper, 1963).

7.   Sigmund Freud, *The Interpretation of Dreams,* trans., James Strachey (New York: Avon Books, 1965) 294-298.

8.   C.G. Jung and Carl Kernyi, *Essays on a Science of Mythology,* trans., R.F.C. Hull (New York: Pantheon books, 1949).

9.   See Otto Rank, *The Myth of the Birth of the Hero,* trans., F. Robbins and Smith Ely Jelliffe, in Rank and others, *In Quest of the Hero* (Princeton: Princeton University Press, 1990) 3-86.

10.   Joseph Campbell, "Folkoristic Commentary" to *Grimm's Fairly Tales,* ed., Joseph Scharl, trans., Margaret Hunt, rev., James Stern (New York: Pantheon, 1943) 841.

11.   See my *Joseph Campbell: An Introduction,* rev. ed. (New York: New American Library, 1990) 61-63.

12.   See ibid. 103-106, 188-193.

13.   See ibid. 126-137.

CHAPTER FOUR

Living Myths

Beverley D. Zabriskie

Archetypal Resonances in Modern Dreams

Snakes slither and rear.

A vulture hovers.

A queenly woman disrobes as she descends the stairs.

An ill man hesitates about intercourse with his mother.

As a woman and her mother open a closet door, the dismembered dummy of a boy falls out. They re-assemble, resew and restuff it.

Through a window, a middle aged woman sees a friend hold the body of her recently dead husband. She suckles him, and he becomes a living baby.

A child is recognized as belonging to the tribe by the cut on his foot.

A female graduate student is provided no chair in the luxurious office of a male teacher. Will she find her own?

A nurse approaches an anxious woman, a feared injection in an enormous needle.

A man who has suffered early rejection feels himself turned to stone. Petrified, his fear impels him to seek help.

As a woman gazes at her reflection in a mirror, her eyes turn green.

A badger appears.

An Indian with a ring in his nose beckons.

On an island between two rivers, guarded by a torch-bearing goddess, at the end of a century and the close of a millennium, these images appeared in the dreams of the nomadic members of many different tribes. The psyches of the late twentieth century settlers in Manhattan—some hunters, some gatherers, some warriors, tricksters, shamans—produced these images, strikingly like those of other peoples and cultures from long ago and far away. An analyst with an archetypal sensibility, even though attending to an individual client in the context of a personal and cultural present, hears echoes from the past, soundings, which orient, signals which guide, announcements which alert both dreamer and listener that an issue has been engaged of such human centrality that the unconscious is speaking from and to this psyche as it has to persons and groups in other crucial times, at crossroads in other places.

A practitioner who approaches and hears these dreams within an archetypal understanding is both alert to their importance for this particular dreamer, and struck by their parallels with the mythic. To interpret these dreams against an archetypal backdrop allows entry to the most deeply personal, and at the same time opens paths to the same wisdom and wonder that impelled and informed world myths. In hearing archetypal resonance, one is impressed by the deeper chords of existential themes beneath a singular melody, as if the exquisite strains of an individual violin are heard with the violas of many cultures and the basses of the human experience itself.

Living Myths

The title of this chapter "Living Myths" suggests a life that is engaged at such depth and individual intensity that it re-embodies that which is most universally human, and re-expresses the stuff of the mythic and imaginal. The phrase also suggests those collective narratives and parables in literature and religion which still live; that is, they carry the power to evoke, to move, to excite, to stir, to disturb, to impel, to soothe. These large myths live when a forceful idea, or a sweeping emotion, seizes and possesses a culture or an individual, whether for a moment or for a millennium.

I hope here to illustrate the psychological role of those living myths, though they be ancient and/or alien, which still appear in contemporary psyches whenever a wider resonance, relevance, and context for one's inner and outer experience is sought or required.

The Psychological Role of Myth

Joseph Campbell, like others such as Sir James Frazer, Robert Briffault, and Mircea Eliade, dedicated himself to finding and presenting humankind's mythic attempts to grasp and comprehend the universe and the meaning of existence in it. Like C.G. Jung and others, he went most deeply into those symbol systems which he loved, which spoke to his own personality, temperament, and beliefs. As a son of the earth, he enlisted the energy of both hunter and gatherer, seeking out particular themes and specific images from many ages and places, collecting his harvest of multiple tales. As a son of the sky, he was drawn by the notion of one universally shared and sheltering myth, and by the possibility of life beyond the galaxy and beyond death.

For those who practice psychotherapy within a Jungian tradition, the images and stories so grandly presented by Campbell are seen as cultural reapings stemming from many individuals' sowings, grand projections of single beams which come from and illuminate individual searches. They are outward cultural expressions which emerge always and everywhere in each generation from what Jung termed the collective unconscious. Campbell's point of the global light shed by myth finds its counterpoint for the Jungian analyst in the light of microscopic sparks of souls. If Campbell the mythologist was fascinated by the inner reaches of outer space, Jung the psychiatrist was charged by the outer reaches of inner space. If Campbell the scholar was drawn to psyche through myth, Jung the analyst was directed toward myth through and for the sake of the psyche which he encountered in those he treated and within himself.

It is of these inner spaces, of the figures, animals, elements, objects which move within that I will speak; I do so not as a mythologist, scholar, or theologian, but as an analyst who daily meets myths through psyche as it lives and appears where the Hudson and the East Rivers meet the sea under a goddess gaze, and where as Campbell once wrote:

> The latest incarnation of Oedipus, the continued romance of Beauty and the Beast, stand this afternoon on the corner of Forty-second Street and Fifth Avenue, waiting for the traffic light to change.[1]

Myth and the Collective Unconscious

At the turn of the century, Sigmund Freud, a neurologist, was exploring the human psyche in Vienna, with a clientele functioning well enough to be living in society and to be seen in a private practice. Dr. Freud saw clients he deemed neurotic, who defended their ego equilibrium largely through the defense of repression, so that disturbing psychic contents, which he believed to be largely sexual in nature, were left forgotten or disguised so as not to threaten the personality. He posited a psychological structure in human beings made up of the collective criteria of the superego, the conscious identity of the ego, and the drives of the id, with threatening memories and traumas stored in the personal unconscious. It was his aim through analysis to make this personal unconscious conscious in a systematic way so that the individual might reclaim memory and experience without destroying the ego's balance. Individuals such as Oedipus, Electra, Moses, and their stories were cited by Freud as analogies and illustrations of primary human situations, as amplifications drawn from history, and world literature.

Jung, on the other hand, a psychiatrist, worked first with hospitalized patients in a clinic near Zurich. Diagnosed as psychotic, as schizophrenic, they used more primitive defenses, and had not achieved the capacity to metabolize trauma or contain the highly charged imagery which arose from their non-ego psyche, the unconscious. He saw the libido as pertaining not only to sex, but to all life drives, including the religious instinct. In attempting to understand the material he met, Jung came to recognize the images emanating in his patients' unconscious as the ancient symbols of mythic and religious systems. He hypothesized that in

addition to the personal unconscious of once known, now re-
pressed memories, there exists in each person a collective unconscious. Here are contained inner versions of cultural themes. He
called the underlying psychological structures of humankind's
over-arching realities archetypes, experienced through the many
images which different peoples and generations fashioned in
order to express the unknown or unknowable. In Jung's understanding the collective unconscious revealed itself individually in
the eruptive imagery of psychotic delusions and the mythpoeic
language of dreams and culturally in religious symbol, ritual
myth, and fairy tale. Since Jung firmly believed in the absolute and
objective reality of the psyche, he viewed the existence of archetypal forms as an undeniable and enduring reality, as aspects of the
"objective psyche," the collective unconscious. He also believed
that this larger than personal unconscious can never be made fully
conscious, for it wells up from a source that is transpersonal and
beyond the individual.

Dreams abound with the same mysteries and enigmas,
chronicles and sagas, saviors and demons, as do epic and rite.
Insofar as all human beings share birth, life, and death, and insofar
as all of us reach the point where the known fears the unknown
(even if the boundary between knowledge and ignorance varies
for different peoples and epochs), our sleeping and waking appre-
hensions and yearnings cluster around the very same questions
and intuitions. No matter who we are when our egos dream, their
defenses against that which might disturb us or threaten us are
weaker, the unconscious stronger.

In tribes and nations, myths were once fashioned and recited
to commemorate and accompany the central rites of passage:
epiphanal moments of genesis (birth) or of emergence out of chaos,
nothingness, or unconsciousness; instances of initiation into conflict or war, solitary trial or ordeal; solemn joinings be they wed-
dings or treaties; peak moments of triumph such as coronations,
conquests, discoveries; in times of defeat, of exile or illness, of
death and burial.[2] They honored beginnings and transformations,
separations and struggles, mortifications and deaths. Marie Louise
von Franz writes in *Creation Myths* that a similar mythic quality is
found in dreams of individuals when there is the potential for new
beginning out of a state of chaos, when the ego is required to get

beyond what is given and established by making a change of attitude, when there is a challenge and opportunity for one who has a constricted self to be initiated, when a creative period or process is about to begin or climax, when one's personality is threatened by physical illness or death, psychological dissolution or breakdown.[3] At such crossroads and passages, ascents and descents, mortifications and resurrections, images similar to those which have emerged from individuals and cultures at parallel points appear. This is not because one's life imitates myth, but because one has met a moment in one's own existence which is as important and as pivotal as the earlier historical event which stimulated myth making. So it was with those persons who dreamt the images mentioned above.

When the outlines of new and renewing life emerge from a person's latest experience of chaos, snakes may slither and slide around one's dreams just as they emerged and were expressed in ancient religious sites such as the Ohio earthworks, a sacred mound and cosmic navel created by a Native American tribe.

When a far reaching and hovering attention is called for, one capable of relating to the deathly for the sake of life, the archaic vulture mother goddess who fed her young on carrion may fly up from the depths.

The woman's descent into a depression beneath the trappings of her worldly persona recalls the Sumerian goddess Innana's journey into the underworld:

> Inanna, from the great above she set her mind
> toward the great below.
> Inanna abandoned heaven, abandoned earth,
> To the nether world she descended.
> Upon her entering the seventh gate, all the
> garments of ladyship of her body were removed.
> What pray is this?

An ill man turns from a death mother who lowers herself on him as the Egyptian sky mother and coffin goddess Nut pressed down upon the deceased.

The two women sew and bind the dummy from the closet, just as the goddesses Isis and Nepthys attended their dismembered brother Osiris:

Ah, Sister, says Isis to Nepthys
This is our brother.
Come, let us lift up his head,
Come, let us rejoin his bones,
Come, let us reassemble his limbs,
Come, let us put an end to all his woes.

The woman's image of her widowed friend, holding her dead husband like the pieta, suckling him as she would a baby, announced to her the possibilities of renewal as she mourned her youth and entered the second half of her life.

A young woman who had been deeply injured as a child has vulnerable and heroic coping energy, like the young Egyptian god Horus, who was able to overcome dark aggression and survive his wound.

The graduate student's dream described her dilemma as the lack of female authority in the image of the missing chair, the goddess throne.

The anxious dreamer is afraid as a nurse comes at her with a hypodermic, yet there is a comfort for her. In Greek myth the personification of health, Hygeia, approached the ill pilgrims in the temple of the healing god Aesclepius, carrying the snake whose bite provided the penetrating cure.

The rejected man, trapped in stone finds his suffering transforms him into a new sense of self, in the tradition of the rejected stone that becomes the key or cornerstone.

The mirror gazing woman looks to herself like the envious stepmother in Snow White.

The man who dreamt of his totem badger and the Indian with the hole in his nose realizes that in the midst of a busy life, he must pursue a quest; he finds himself in Oregon, following the trail of the Nez Pierce, the nose-pierced Indian Chief Joseph, he who declared: I will fight no more forever.

Numinous Images

While these images belong to no specific dogma, nor have dogmatic purpose, they nonetheless impart a numinous or religious quality. They have the effect of linking and binding the dreamer to otherness, first to an otherness within, to non-ego parts of psyche, then to the otherness of culture, race, species, and ultimately to the numinous otherness of the extra-human, the transpersonal and transcendent. They are not sectarian; rather, they alert and sensitize the individual to the underlying archetypal realities which lie beneath cultural and religious manifestations. They offer access to many forms of human experience, and for some people, being freed from one structure allows an openness to the religious dimension of many phenomena—met within and without—to develop. The synthesis or co-existence of forms may then carry a broader numinosity and provide the person a wider opening to the transcendent. Perhaps, as Campbell's appeal and this volume attest, there are many who are receptive to the glimpses of the unseeable offered by different traditions. Each one weaves a strand in the mythpoeic net to widen our grasp of the fabric of existence. Here is an interesting example of a synthesis of forms and imagery. In an artistic drawing a priest turned toward the congregation making the solemn gesture of benediction in the name of the father, son, and holy ghost. The congregation responded, however, with the graceful gesture of the yin and yang of a Tai Chi movement.

The Challenge of the Mythic Approach

Is this mythic and psychological approach a danger to the prevailing religions of our western tradition? Toward the end of his life Jung wrote:

> These melting processes all express a relativization of the dominants of consciousness prevailing in a given age. For those who identify with the dominants or are absolutely dependent on them, the melting process appears as a hostile, destructive attack, which should be resisted with all one's powers. Others, for whom the dominants no longer mean what they purport to be, see the melting as a longing for regeneration and enrichment of a system of ideas that has lost its vitality and freshness and is already obsolete. The melting process is either something very bad or something highly desirable, according to the observer's standpoint.

One of my critics includes me among the smelters on the ground that I take an interest in the psychology of comparative religion. This is justified insofar as I have called all religious ideas psychic (though their possible transcendental meaning is something I am not competent to judge). I maintain that there is a relationship between Christian doctrine and psychology. If Christian doctrine is able to assimilate the fateful impact of psychology that is a sign of vitality, for life is assimilation. Anything that ceases to assimilate dies.[4]

If we respect the validity of many different avenues toward transcendent meaning, the worth of one's own faith or philosophy need not depend on the annihilation of another belief. Nor need we use history and politics to act out our mythic projections or anxieties.

Attention to the myths of a society often sheds light on that society's historical development: In terms of one of the most recent historical mythic eruptions, the Holocaust, might one see it in part as the horrific enmity of the Germanic sky god culture for the older Hebraic sky god civilization? Might not that inhuman nightmare have been prevented if more people had understood what was happening? What if they had been able to see that a mythic possession was taking place in which one people identified themselves with the superman and were afflicted by a mythic dread of an ultimate *Götterdämmerung* which they themselves inflicted upon another race, which was awaiting not destruction by the gods but the coming of a saving messiah? Would we so easily have acquiesced as a nation to our recent blanket bombing of another people, were it not that deep in our psyches there lurks remnants of the sentiments of Revelation 17:5: "On her forehead was written a symbolic name, 'Babylon the great, mother of harlots and all the world's abomination.'"

Different Approaches to Myth

It is perhaps true that the mythologist and the analyst approach myth differently. Does the analyst agree with Campbell's "Follow your bliss"? Jung might say one must follow its opposite as well; we should follow our fear, our anxieties, our conflicts, our sufferings, our tears. Follow our projections, our complexes. Follow our symptoms, our sores, and our defeats, because if we note our ego's defeats we are reminded of that which is larger than ourselves, the transcendent energy that Jung called the Self. We should pursue our darkness and our shadows until we locate them within. We should follow not only our dreams but our nightmares so that we will not make others' lives into nightmares.

As in every human endeavor, in our romance with myth, whether in the tradition of Jung or of Campbell, there surely works the shadow, which we must pursue lest it cast itself around and through us. We must be alert to this because an openness to the universals can co-exist with prejudice toward personal difference, concentration on the grand can neglect the small, the penchant to organize a whole can reductively categorize the parts, a penchant for archetypes can reify in stereotypes.

The Advantage of Engaging Myths

Still, through authentic self-recognition in myth, we may live lives of wonder and humility, dissolving self importance (which often masks a failure to see ourselves as significant), healing the wounds from past diminishment and devaluation, countering the pull toward isolation and narcissism. Exposure to myth can address one's need for kinship, and one's desire to be oriented to something outside and larger than oneself. Indeed, it may determine the state of our souls, for, as Jung wrote:

> Collective ideals are not by a long way the breath of life which a man needs in order to live. If his soul does not live nothing can save him from stultification. His life is the soil in which his soul can and must develop. He has only the mystery of his living soul to set against the overwhelming might and brutality of collective convictions.[5]

Like the contribution of other mythologists and interpreters, Campbell's work helps one to find the imagistic and poetic wisdom of the generations. When engaged with intelligently, it encourages us to place ourselves in the larger context of our humanity, beyond the social strata of our egos which are bound by time and place. It also serves to free ourselves and our cultures from compulsive repetitions of the past, which could cause us to spend lifetimes living our myths rather than our individual human lives. We are fully human not only if we know our myths and relate to them, but also if we know our myths and *disidentify* from them.

The retelling of humankind's central and recurring tales touches deep chords, the same ones played by any metaphysic, religion or metapsychology that rings true, because the mythic symbols and images ask the large questions and offer possible, if partial, answers to the concerns of all whose lives are greater than the givens of biological existence.

Involvement with dreams and myths is not escape, not avoidance. They point the dreamer both more deeply into the self, and through and beyond the self to our fellows, our culture, our world. For as Jung writes,

> Self-knowledge is an adventure that carries us unexpectedly far and deep. Self-knowledge is not an isolated process; it is possible only if the reality of the world around us is recognized.[6]

Dreams and myths allow the woman or man who knows their presence both to value more proudly what a single individual suffers and to accept more humbly that which is only and altogether human.

> In the face of huge numbers, every thought of individuality pales, for statistics obliterate everything unique. Contemplating such overwhelming might and misery, the individual is embarrassed to exist at all. Yet the real carrier of life is the individual. He alone feels happiness. He alone has virtue and responsibility and any ethics whatever. The masses and the state have nothing of the kind. Only man as an individual human being lives[7]

The sounding of an archetypal theme in an experience or dream can release an individual from denial, isolation, and shame, and lead them into engagement, compassion and celebration. Above all, myth allows us to see, to recognize ourselves and others within a larger and longer reality.

The latest incarnation of Oedipus, the continued romance of Beauty and the Beast, stand this afternoon on the corner of Forty-second Street and Fifth Avenue, waiting for the traffic light to change.[8]

Meanwhile, the lady of the sinking spirits, descending the stairs in the nearby building, feels as stripped as Inanna. Next door, a graduate student, completing her thesis defense feels as solid in her newly won authority as the goddess throne. In the hospital uptown, a doctor wearing a badge of Asclepius' cadeuscus, asks his Hygeia-like colleague for her healing attention to one who lies ill. A mother in the house around the corner, reflects on her more shadowy self, faces her envy of her beautiful Snow White daughter. A young survivor, as wounded by hostile forces as was Horus, recognizes a kindred spirit by the look of determination in his eyes. A white man, at a moment of outer defeat and inner dignity, recognizes his kinship with the red man and identifies with the feeling "I will fight no more forever." Another, hoping to be an eagle, accepts his way is like that of the badger—biting and chewing away, bit by bit, but inexorably. They—we—proceed proudly with life. They—we—carry forth the myths of old, even as daily we shape the new.

NOTES

1. Joseph Campbell, *Hero with a Thousand Faces* (Princeton: Princeton University Press, 1968) 4.

2. David Adams Lemming, *The World of Myth* (New York: Oxford University Press, 1990).

3. Marie Louise von Franz, *Creation Myths* (Zurich: Spring Publications, 1972).

4. C.C. Jung, *Mysterium* (Princeton: Princeton University Press, 1970).

5. Ibid. 165.

6. Ibid. 520.

7. Ibid. 163.

8. Campbell, *Hero* 4.

CHAPTER FIVE

A Theologian's "Hero's Journey" into Joseph Campbell:

the Man, the Scholar, the Myth

Peter E. Fink, S.J.

I'd like to take you on a journey with me into the world of Joseph Campbell. It is a journey guided by the interests, the concerns, and at times the wonders of a Catholic theologian, namely, myself. The language of the journey, and even its shape, come, of course, from the man we explore. Joseph Campbell will be both guide along the quest and the quest itself.

The method of exploration is based on a hunch that has so far been borne out in a variety of conversations which I have had with others about Joseph Campbell. The hunch is that if one wants to approach what Joseph Campbell has to offer, and if one wants to understand the chords which he has struck in popular consciousness, more will be found by taking a journey into what he has done, than by an objective analysis of his works. The central question for me is not so much what Joseph Campbell has to say, which can only be answered by listening to him directly, but rather what Joseph Campbell has to offer between, around, and in the midst of the many things he says. We are examining "the phenomenon of Joseph Campbell"; we ask why he has claimed the interest of so many thoughtful religious people who find him both fascinating and irritating, intriguing and frustrating, and for all that, someone who captures their imagination and will not let go.

First, some personal biography. My primary theological interest in myth and symbol has to do with the role that these play in the narrative and ritual structures of Christian worship. On this level alone I find the Joseph Campbell phenomenon a challenge. It is humbling to watch this weaver of myth and story succeed in awakening life in his listeners while we who deal professionally in the myths and stories of Christian ritual do not. Yet if the truth be told, I find that Campbell has intrigued and challenged me on a much deeper level than just my area of professional concern. I am caught up in his work and himself, not only as a sacramental-liturgical theologian, but as a person, a priest and a Roman Catholic believer as well. This man who left the church, and who has spent much energy in critical dialogue with things of the church, has nonetheless insights into the church which I need to listen to and attend to.

I could, of course, stand back at a distance and make scholarly observations about the man and his works, but that, I fear, would have only limited yield. If I want to find out what chords he strikes in others I have to begin with the chords he strikes in me, and try to find out what they are. Whether or not they are the same chords for anyone else, can only be discovered as those chords are uncovered and named.

There is a preliminary question that needs to be asked before the journey begins. It is clear that there is a Joseph Campbell phenomenon. What a theologian has to ask about this phenomenon is what makes it theologically interesting? It is not enough to note that Campbell deals with religious or theological material, or even that he makes theological statements. The phenomenon is interesting theologically only to the extent that it arises from a realm of human experience where knowledge and love of God are found, and only to the extent that it addresses and illuminates that same realm of human experience. Campbell himself, and not only the myths he deals with, speaks of that holy mystery with which theology is concerned, a mystery that at one and the same time resides in the depth of human life and is nonetheless experienced as transcendent of human life. The theologian's question, or at least this theologian's question, is this: What aspects of the mystery do Joseph Campbell and the Joseph Campbell phenomenon unveil?

But now to the matter at hand. The title I have chosen for this essay is: A Theologian's "Hero's Journey" into Joseph Campbell:

the Man, the Scholar, the Myth. My use of Campbell's "hero's journey" is not an attempt to be clever. It accurately describes what I think is the most appropriate way to engage the richness Campbell offers. On the hero's journey, one leaves the world of the familiar and travels into a world that is fraught with risk, and yet a world which holds promise of something, perhaps wisdom, perhaps knowledge that is "saving knowledge." It is a world that will yield a "boon" for those whom the hero leaves behind if and when the hero should return.

While Campbell's own hero has a thousand faces, the term "hero" as I use it here has at least two: Campbell's and mine. But as I take you along this theologian's journey with me, I invite you to become a bit of the hero yourself. Enter the journey with me, and do some of your own wondering along the way.

The rest of the title names, in the right order, both the levels on which Campbell has claimed my attention, and the levels of the journey before us. It was the man first before the scholar that drew me in. Now more than either of these two, it is Joseph Campbell the mythic figure who fascinates me. And because he has become somewhat of a mythic figure for me and for so many others, his secrets are dislodged by engaging him as one would a myth rather than by studying his works as one would the works of a scholar.

I tend to read Campbell, as I do all myths and symbols, through the eyes of one of my great intellectual heros, Paul Ricoeur. In Ricoeur's language, Joseph Campbell, the man, presents a first naiveté. One can be mesmerized, even seduced, by him. Passage into Joseph Campbell the scholar involves a bit of a loss of innocence. His words do not always stand up well to critique, and the very things that initially seduce can in the end evoke a variety of negative reactions. It is amazing to me the levels of anger which Campbell, the scholar, can summon up in other scholars. But the anger itself is interesting because it doesn't allow these people to let go of Campbell. Even when they are furious there is something about him that claims and holds their attention. It is that "something" which I maintain is what Campbell really has to offer. To find that something, again in Ricoeur's language, one must move beyond the loss of innocence to the second naiveté. One must move, therefore, beyond Campbell the scholar to Campbell the symbol, Campbell the myth. The "hero's journey" I invite you along is then a journey through a loss of innocence to the second naiveté.

Beginning

The name Joseph Campbell had been long known to me as someone whose works "I'd someday like to read." Some of those works were on my shelf. I even began several of the volumes of *Masks of God* and several chapters of *Hero* several times. But I can't say he grabbed me until I first encountered him in the PBS tapes, the single on the "Hero's Journey" and the six-episode "The Power of Myth."

I caught the single when I was on sabbatical in Hawaii, where I was already attuned to the mythic imagination in a more than ordinary way. I used to watch the mountains of the Ko'olau range on Oahu and the clouds which interacted with them. I found myself describing this interaction in terms of human affection: "the clouds are angry," "the two of them are being playful," "the mountains are resisting the clouds' erotic advances," etc. It was the first time I had ever done that. I found myself understanding how myths are born in a way I never had, or at least never noticed. And Hawaii is definitely a land where myths are born.

Right before I went to Hawaii, when I was in San Francisco in January, 1988 for the annual meeting of the North American Academy of Liturgy, I came upon a sizeable obituary of Campbell written by a woman named Joan Marler in the program guide for KPFA and KFCF in San Francisco. Hers was a reflective piece that captured in good summary fashion most of the key insights which Campbell brought forth. It also was a witness to the chords which Campbell struck in her and in many others besides. As I reread it recently with this essay in mind, I found myself resonating with her tribute and being drawn by way of recollection into Campbell, his tapes and his works once again. Let me recite some of them here, and comment upon them, invite you to resonate with them, for I think they will take us a bit closer to some of the "chords" which Campbell still strikes in many of us.

She recalled that Campbell was "discovered" in the 1960s "by a generation of individuals seeking a more profound perspective on the meaning of life than the ossified images of Western religion provided." I would qualify that only by adding that Campbell was less interested in the "meaning of life" than he was in the "experience of being alive"—which is probably true of the 1960s as well. But this is a primary chord which Campbell strikes. That sound byte, "the experience of being alive," touches a deep yearning in myself and in so many others with whom I have enjoyed conversation.

Joan Marler continued with the observation that the concept of the heroic quest struck a deep chord in many who were able to perceive their own inner search within a universal context. There is no doubt that the "inner search" continues to be an alive contemporary quest. The mappings of such inner quest are legion: the INFP-ESTJ of Myers-Briggs, the enneagram nine going on three, several stages of faith development, language of co-dependency and dysfunctionality. In a recent seminar, which I'll describe later, the participants all began hoping to find a new mapping in the works of Campbell—certainly they were looking for someone new to help in their own personal quest.

What was intriguing, however, was how quickly the language of personal quest and inner search became a source of discomfort for everyone in the group. In part the discomfort came because "personal quest" seemed too solipsistic; in part because it has become so identified with popular forms of psychology that take people into their own guts and seemingly leave them there. As one of them put it: the journey inward has got to be more serious than that, and has got to yield something more promising than simply the dead end of solitary self-discovery.

It is there I began to think that perhaps the interest in Campbell is not a one-level interest, and that Campbell himself, while seducing us by an initial appeal to the self-quest, sooner or later exposes that quest to a shallowness that finally makes it unsatisfactory. I have no doubt that for many the initial appeal of Campbell is very shallow. But if that were all, it would be too short lived to be humanly interesting, much less theologically interesting. It becomes interesting on both the human and the theological level when Campbell himself exposes the shallowness and invites the journeyer to discover deeper levels of oneself, others and the mystery which symbol and myth bring forth.

There was a third point Marler made about Campbell: "While other scholars were emphasizing the infinite variations of mythical expression," she wrote, "Campbell noticed similarities . . . (that) there are basic underlying mythological themes or 'elemental ideas' which are constant throughout time and space, regardless of local variations." I think one of his strong appeals, at least to me, has to do with the challenge he brings to the issue of how we treat differences. He seems to indicate that differences should be seen not necessarily as alienating one thing from another, but rather as capable of contributing to the understanding of one another.

A fourth point. Citing Campbell, Marler notes that "until recently, the cultural horizons of most societies were stable and finite. The individuals who ventured beyond the accepted world view and social order to discover the mythic and psychological ground of their own being did so only of their own accord. These were the shamans, and the creative outcasts. But today, that perilous adventure comes to everybody because the world is in such a state of flux." But that is only in part Campbell's view. The other part, which Marler does not cite, is Campbell's reminder that not everyone is up to the task, and that there is a danger of trivializing the task out of some false sense of egalitarianism. When everyone must be a shaman, the shaman's task gets reduced to what everyone can do. Reduced, and perhaps lost in the process.

A Catholic theologian cannot help but think of one aspect of contemporary church life. The shamans in the church are few and far between. And the church, like the world, is in a state of flux. Its official guides seem more intent on controlling the flux than on guiding people through it. Perhaps Campbell intrigues people in a way that official religion today does not because he himself is a bit of the shaman. He certainly ventured beyond the accepted religious world view and social order and discovered the rich mythic and psychological ground of all being in a way and in a place quite outside the structured religious world of his own upbringing. But he is more than a rebel and more than a wanderer. He is in the way of the shaman a speaker of truth, and truth has a way of claiming the human heart.

A fifth observation made by Marler comes to focus on what is perhaps Campbell's most well known phrase: "follow your bliss." It is at once a dangerous and enticing phrase. The context of the phrase is a conflict within the human person, the ever-widening split between mind and body. Elemental ideas lead us inward, but our minds lead us outward into interests not necessarily consonant with the urges of our bodies. It is to mend this split that Campbell urges, "follow your bliss."

There are two elements to note in this connection. The first is the obvious, and yet dangerous, appeal in the phrase, "follow your bliss." It appeals to the bored, the confused, the aimless, the frightened, the controlled, the manipulated: in short, all of us. And it touches that same chord which the ancient words of Irenaeus continue to touch: "the glory of God is the human person fully alive." And yet it is dangerous. It sounds too much like the contemporary "do your own thing," which on a superficial level at least has shown itself to be very destructive. The second element to note is the importance of the challenge to overcome the body-mind split especially where mind and body take us in different directions in regard, say, to sexuality, ecology, war and peace, issues of justice, to name only a few. This is a challenge already being embraced by theologians all across the board. There is deep appeal in this challenge.

One last insight from this quite pregnant obituary of Joseph Campbell. Marler says: Joseph Campbell saw that we are in an entirely new era in human history, and it is time to rediscover an experience of the entire earth as the holy land, here and now. "If we do not love the earth, and identify with it, we may not survive . . . It is one humankind . . . The first function of mythology is to open the mind to the mystery of the universe, the mystery of one's self . . ." I think this vision of the one earth and the one humanity is equally as powerful as, if not even more powerful than, the more individual "follow your bliss," and challenges as superficial any view of one's bliss that is anywhere near the same as "doing one's own thing."

All of the above, the PBS tapes, the experience of Hawaii and that wonderful obituary of Campbell which I simply happened upon, mark but the beginning of the journey. Let me continue with Campbell's "journey" language and speak about the "summons."

Summons

I use the word "summons" to identify the more immediate occasion for the journey, namely, the specific chords which Campbell strikes in me. He is, as I say, more than just interesting. The allure he has which amounts to a summons to me has to do with an interest I have had in developing an indigenous North American theology. There is a potential promise offered by Campbell in this regard.

For a long time U.S. theology has borrowed from Europe. More recently there has been a shift in the borrowing to Latin America and other "third-world" places where liberation theology has taken hold. While I appreciate some of the thrust of liberation theology, I am not sure how well it translates into English speaking North America. As I understand its origin, it is born in segments of the third world where faith struggles to deal with poverty, oppression, and other crass social and political realities. It is born, as theology must be, in faith. When it crosses the "gringo" border, however, it seems to transmute itself into political ideology rather than theology. Whether it be "gay liberation," or "black liberation," or "women's liberation," the aim is clear; what is not clear is the faith required for liberation to be liberation theology.

While I strongly believe that in a solid liberation theology the reality of the poor, the oppressed, and the marginalized is the place to begin, and while I am quite convinced that this same reality must be included in a U.S./North American theology as well, I am not sure that in a "first world" theology the poor and the marginalized can be the place to begin. And I begin to wonder if the Joseph Campbell phenomenon, which portrays the power of myth to excite and awaken faith and hope and love in the middle and upper classes might hold a clue to a more promising starting point. We are not without a history of mythic structures that have guided both the religious and political dimensions of our culture. These traditional structures, however, seem to have run aground. What is needed is for religious faith to articulate and ground new

mythic structures both in challenge to current church and govern-
ment policies and as a force to guide them into the future. The
hopes of the wealthy as well as the poor must be included in such
new mythic structures.

Where Joseph Campbell offers both help and challenge is in
the distinction he draws between true myths and pseudo-myths,
namely, non-myths pretending to serve as myth but without the
healing power which true myths contain. Unfortunately, our own
U.S. American culture has far more pseudo-myths in operation
than true liberating myths. A good example of pseudo-myth can
be found in any television mini-series, where all human realities
are resolved in five or six segments, and where human realities
that are tragic or horrifying or simply repulsive become instead
the evening's entertainment. The recent Gulf War, for example,
became for many people more exciting than tragic; some lurid
murder cases play on the television news like an Agatha Christie
mystery. One might wonder the same about the "greenhouse
effect," the frightening reality of AIDS, poverty in Ethiopia, war in
Central America, even volcanic eruption in the Philippines. The
mini-series is really pseudo-myth because it does not open the
world of terror to wisdom but rather turns the world of terror into
entertainment. The challenge which Campbell brings to us as we
experience the terrors of life is the challenge to enter them and
there to find wisdom once again.

The second chord of wonder is not independent of the first;
perhaps the difference is that it touches a pastoral as well as a
theological chord. There was an "op-ed" piece by Christopher
Lasch in the New York Times, Dec. 29, 1989 entitled: "The I's Have
It for Another Decade." Let me cite some parts of it, again in the
hope that it will pluck some chords in ourselves.

Speaking about the "end of the me-decade" which did not
come about, Lasch says: "Americans in the 80's devoted themselves more single-mindedly than ever to self-enrichment and self
gratification." But, "selfishness, me-ism, yuppie greed . . . do not
describe very clearly what ails us. The moral bottom has dropped
out of our culture. Americans have no compelling incentive to
postpone gratification, because they no longer believe in the
future . . . The dream of a better world collapsed in the late 60s, and
nothing has taken its place."

This is certainly a chilling indictment, but one which I am not about to deny. My wonder as theologian and pastor is: has Joseph Campbell suggested a solution to this emptiness? Do we find in his words and his wonderings the promise of something that will take the place of our culture's old dreams?

Lasch goes on to say: "I believe that young people in our society are living in a state of almost unbearable . . . agony. They experience the world only as a source of pleasure and pain. The culture . . . provides so little help in ordering the world that experience comes to them in the form merely of direct stimulation or deprivation, without much symbolic mediation." He sees little difference here between the young in the suburbs and those in the ghetto, both are equally hopeless. Again I wonder, is this where Joseph Campbell has struck a chord? Does Campbell offer hope to the hopeless?

Lasch's final observation concerns what he calls our failure to provide the young with a culture that claims to explain the world or that links their experience with those that came before or those who will follow. This, he says, was once the role of "stories," that is, bible stories, classical myths, fairy tales, patriotic legends. We all had them in common. "If you take away that background, the foreground fills the whole picture—an insistent 'I want.'" Is this what Joseph Campbell meant when in responding to Bill Moyer's question, "What happens when myths disappear," he said, "Look at the newspapers."

A sense of the past and the future, a sense of continuity with people past and people present, a sense of a context for living—all of which myth provides—seems to be desperately needed by people today. Religion doesn't seem to be answering the need, nor the philosophy behind politics and public policy. The moral bottom seems to have dropped out. Here Campbell challenges us to ask: what myths will serve the future? But another question is equally challenging: why do we delight in and dole out pseudo-myths? Is it possible that pseudo-myths seem to give us control over the outcome of events and over people that engagement with real myths does not give?

The final element that has the character of a summons for me is the quality of the man himself. The video interviews with

Campbell, more than his written works, awakened something in me which I wanted to understand. This is why I find it important to begin with Campbell the man before going on to Campbell the scholar. I don't think Joseph Campbell's power can be divorced from the intriguing person and his personal depth that comes to light poignantly in the Bill Moyer's interviews with him. As I said above, he is a speaker of truth, and truth has a way of claiming the human heart. And the truth which he speaks is less a matter of what he says, than what he *sees*. I think what fascinates me most about Campbell has to do with what he sees. I'll come back to this below, because I think this might be my own deepest response to Campbell. He sees something I don't see; I want to see it too. Or maybe the truth is that I *do* see it, and am fascinated that he has the courage to name it.

At any rate, here is where the triptych comes in, and where the journey itself begins to take shape: the man tells me who is speaking; the scholar tells me what he says; but the myth unveils to me something of what he sees.

Journey

In this third section, I will try to take you on a journey by describing another journey already taken. The original journey unfolded over the course of a semester in a seminar I led with thirteen other participants at Weston School of Theology, Cambridge, Massachusetts, entitled "Faith, and the Power of Myth."

Presenting the Journey

I proposed to the Weston class two ways of conducting a seminar: (1) the analytic approach which would study and critique Campbell's writings; (2) a conversational approach which would hold Campbell as a dialogue partner along the path of our own quests and questions. I urged the second as the better way to engage mythic materials and as the way Campbell himself would probably recommend be followed.

I proposed three questions for the seminar conversations: (1) what is the relationship between the mythic imagination and religious faith; (2) what is the role of myth in the genesis of a U.S./ North American theology; and, (3) what is the nature of "The Joseph Campbell phenomenon." On the third, I operated from a premise that Campbell communicates a vitality in religious myth and symbol that we custodians of same yearn to discover and communicate. As I mentioned earlier, I think this is in part why theology students and liturgy folks find Campbell so inviting and challenging.

In the seminar we would have to remember that different rules govern conversation in contrast to critical analysis. In conversation disagreements abound, and critique, if noted, is usually secondary or irrelevant. In analysis, points of disagreement easily become the central focus. A good conversation should turn each of us back to our own quest, taking up what makes a positive contribution and leaving behind what does not. In a conversational approach, each quest will be different though in dialogue with the same partner. In an analytic approach the quest would be the same and the partners follow it together.

Finally, I adapted a distinction Campbell makes between seeking the meaning of life and seeking the experience of being alive. For our seminar, I proposed a distinction between the meaning of faith and the experience of believing. The experience of believing was held out as the goal of our quest.

The Journey Itself

Certain readings were required before each seminar session. Also, at every session some portion of the video series, "The Power of Myth" was viewed; this triggered the conversation more than the readings. Each week each student wrote a single page of observations based on the development of their own quest. I took "quotes" from these each week and fed them back to the group to help guide and direct our conversation. From time to time I introduced some other ideas such as Ricoeur's symbolism, John Macmurray's personal knowledge, and helpful schematics on the development and decline of institutions. I asked the students to keep watch over what readings or other speculations they were guided to as our conversations proceeded. My premise here was that in engaging Campbell they would find things awakening in their imaginations, and these should not be lost, but preserved. I, myself, was led to more of Bill Moyers work (the "World of Ideas" tapes), a book on Gaia consciousness, some readings in ecology, issues of globalization, to name just some. I considered this more important than the "required readings" which were prepared before the conversations began.

The first stage in the student's journey consisted in a fascination and an enthusiasm with Campbell. This was to be expected since an interest in Campbell is what brought them to the seminar in the first place. The language used here was of becoming "unstuck": they experienced having a sense of largeness, of freedom, of simple admiration of the scope of things that they were being invited into. It was, to use Campbell's own term, a "boon" being offered which was seen to be desirable.

The second stage arrived more quickly than I had expected. In a matter of weeks all hell broke loose. There was a good deal of frustration with Campbell's elusiveness and what seemed to be at times his incredible "slight-of-hand." Many of the women found his male dominated approach to myths simply offensive. I found this fascinating because Campbell himself maintained that his Sarah Lawrence students (all women) taught him to view myths through feminine eyes. We all spotted and resisted his anti-Catholic, anti-Christian bias. The church he was still fighting against was a church that many of my students never even knew, and whose passing I myself never lamented. His alleged anti-semitism which has been hotly debated in other group's discussions of Campbell did not arise in the seminar conversations.

At that point of high frustration and even fury, the group would have been delighted to take him on, and thus to slip into the analytic, non-conversational mode. At this point I suggested that we acknowledge our resistance to him, go on with the conversations and the quest, and let the resistance itself be a factor in the conversations.

Several manifestations of the power of myth began to surface as the dialogue continued. These can best be given by a few of the "quotes."

> As I begin to examine my own journey in terms of what I am being exposed to in this course, I feel as though I'm gaining entry into a whole other dimension of experience that has lain dormant for me. This dimension pulls me out of myself.

... the myth of the hero touches no chord in me. The individualism, the separation, the lonely return hold little attraction to me. However, when I read what in its earliest form seems to be a "woman's myth," I see that the individual and the community form a relationship of interdependence so that what affects one affects the other ... This sense of being drawn in is something I want to attend to ...

... a call to identification with ...

The power of myth ... lies in its ability to stir the truth that sleeps within each human person. For a brief moment we taste the freedom such awakening of truth reveals. We are filled with an excitement characterized by energizing hope and terrifying fear. The inner liberation experienced launches us on a journey that is at once life-giving and fear-filled.

A myth is a story which connects me with the flow of my own unfolding life process ... I get attached to the hero/heroine. Once I am completely identified with the hero/ine, I come to realize that what I am fascinated with and what I love in the other is really part of myself that I had only partially encountered before, or not at all.

We went on to talk about "types" of myths: redemption myths, sacrifice myths, myths of bliss and ecstasy. It was noted that Christianity has an abundance of redemption and sacrifice myths, but relatively few myths of ecstasy—which might be why the affection of true eucharistia is so hard to come by. It might also have something to do with the frequent joylessness of so many Christian liturgies. This paucity of ecstasy myths also posed a problem with our dealing with Campbell's flagship phrase: "Follow your bliss." Is it possible that "bliss" can only be read superficially when it has no strong myths of ecstasy and eucharistia to shore it up.

In a turn that was surprising to me, a relatively old bit of Christian wisdom surfaced without qualm or hesitation when we took both myths of bliss and of sacrifice beyond their surface; there one discovered that the promise of bliss gives motive for sacrifice, and that sacrifice is the path to bliss. If I had begun the course with such a blithe statement, I suspect the students would have rejected it. What made them accept it now? The crucial turn seemed to come when the journey into myths of either kind clearly became a relational journey, a journey that necessarily involved others. Here is how one participant phrased it:

> This was my experience so far in this course: I focused first of all on my attempt to seek fulfillment and self-understanding by looking at what myths I live by. That at the time seemed important and exciting. But now I (and I think we) have turned to seek something more, something which is outside of the self, something which encompasses the self, and which we have in common. I think this is a necessary course of events, if we are true to the search, because, in the end, bliss is sacrifice (self-offering) and sacrifice is bliss.

What surfaced here is not only the danger of a superficial reading of myths, but the need to continually push one's engagement with myths to deeper and deeper levels. Myths that seem disparate at first, or even conflictual, become on deeper levels shadow sides of each other, and until that deeper level is reached, the engagement with the myth risks falsifying the mythic truth rather than unveiling it. It may well be that the real problem with so many religious myths today is not that they no longer speak, but rather that they have been rendered false by a superficial reading of them.

Campbell's statement that "all religions are true" is a good case in point. On a very superficial level it may be appealing to the disenchanted; to the religiously committed it is simple heresy. Yet what happens when one goes deeper into the myths that are proper to the various religions? Do they not all lead, as Karl Rahner says, to the ineffable one to whom even the most personally sacred myths can only point. One must go deeper into the various myths to find the level where there is truth to Campbell's statement. But such a journey requires a Campbell "hero" because for much must be surrendered along the way. I sometimes wonder if Campbell himself has really gone that far?

At this point in the journey the questions shifted somewhat from dealing with the power of myth to dealing with the power of the myth-maker. A large part of the power of myth, we mused, lies in the hands of a true myth-maker who has the ability to speak from inside the myth. Part of the power also lies, it was suggested, in the involvement of one's whole body in telling the myth. Reference was made to the character Robin Williams played in the film "Dead Poets Society." That teacher of poetry in a boy's prep school was truly a "myth-maker," one who clearly had the power to bring story to life from the written page. For him the human body held great power; he had the boys lean into the school's trophy case as he told of the past, he had them stand on their desk to see the world differently, and, of course, at the end of the film, when words failed, they stood on their desks in tribute to him. Such use of the body and bodily animation was also noted in the Moyer/Campbell tapes as a source of significant power to bring myth to life. Even when Campbell was simply sitting down, his body was doing more than sitting down.

From this point on in the journey the power of myth and the power of the myth-maker became intertwined. Campbell himself surfaced as a powerful myth-maker who spoke from the inside of the myths that his own scholarly work introduced him to. It is in this sense that Campbell the man and the scholar himself became the myth, and we realized we had been taking a "hero's journey" into him to discover the boon he offered. We realized too that we had to leave behind many things: the security of the analytic mode so common to academe, our own needs for sure comprehension, our own "safe distance." And we discovered that the challenges which faced us on our collective "hero's journey" were, as Campbell predicted, challenges in ourselves.

This took us closer and closer to the boon, which at this point we were still naming: to see what he sees.

Boon

We turned finally to a discussion of the boon of our journey. It had become clear by this time that Campbell the myth-maker, more than the myths he recounted, had captured our attention. I found myself thinking of that wonderful summation of the art of preaching given by Walter Burghardt in his essay, "The Word Made Flesh Today," from the collection *Tell the Next Generation: Homilies and Near Homilies:* "... ultimately I am the word, the word that is heard ... The word is ... I."[1]

Campbell not only speaks about the hero's journey; clearly he has taken it himself. Though he preferred to think of himself as a maverick rather than as a hero, his life did follow the hero's path. And as we listen to him, we sense a boon that is offered as a result of his journey. I say to myself, "He knows something I don't know, and I want to find out what it is; he sees something I don't see, and I want to see it myself."

What none of us realized until toward the end of the seminar was that we too had to follow the hero's path, this time into Campbell himself, in order to discover the boon. And we discovered something else as well: the boon is not adequately or accurately named as seeing what he saw. There was still too much resistance to what he saw, or at least to his naming of what he saw. The real boon, beyond resistance and beyond disagreement with his own naming of things, was rather to see as he sees.

And here finally we sat around the fire at journey's end. Three things surfaced at the deepest level to name the appeal most of us found in dialoging with Joseph Campbell: beauty, passion, and freedom. The panorama of religious myth which Campbell sets out is certainly beautiful. But more than that, he speaks as one who has seen "the beautiful" and who is himself beautiful in the speaking. In addition, Campbell was seen to be a man of both passion and freedom. The experience of being alive is an experience of passion and of freedom. The chords he struck in my students are passion and freedom. The chords that inspired all sorts of resistance were passion and freedom. And after it all the words Joseph Campbell still speaks to me are passion and freedom. Beyond any superficial reading of "following one's bliss," lie passion and freedom, the true secret of "one's bliss."

* * * * * *

Now, what do I hope you shall make of all of this? I do not really hope at the end of it that you agree with me. I hope you don't disagree with me, of course. But agreement or disagreement is ultimately beside the point. Passion and freedom touch yearnings that are very deep in me, and they have worn many faces in my own personal, scholarly, and maybe even mythic life. I hope these words touch chords equally alive in you.

But a lot will depend on how you hear what I have said. If you hear it in the analytical mode, your own reactions will keep you in the analytic: you will be thinking of the truth or falsehood of what I have said, and rummaging in your mind over the various works of Joseph Campbell to assess things. That is not a bad place to be nor a bad thing to do. If that happens, however, I am not sure I will have served Campbell or us well. As I have presented the man, the scholar, and the myth, I have tried myself to speak as a myth-maker. Or maybe as a hero with a very small "h". The value of my remarks, and the value of my very small journey into Joseph Campbell, man, scholar, myth, lies in the chords that have been struck in you as you have been reading.

I began all this by noting that my professional interest in myth and symbol is the role that they play in the narrative and ritual structures of Christian worship. One thing I am sure of: myth needs the myth-maker to tell it, symbols need the symbol maker to succeed and ritual needs the ritual maker to serve it. All three need women and men who can bring them to life by going where Joseph Campbell has gone: into the myth, the symbol, the ritual. And this "going into" is not a strictly academic pursuit. It requires a hero's journey, so that the energy of the myth, the symbol and the ritual may come from the journey itself, and itself be the primary boon which myth-makers, symbol-makers and ritual makers may offer to others on their return.

* * * * * *

I asked at the very beginning why the Joseph Campbell phe-nomenon might be theologically interesting, and ventured there that "the phenomenon is interesting theologically to the extent that it arises from a realm of human experience where knowledge and love of God are found." In a Christian anthropology guided by Karl Rahner, that "holy mystery" is named as the horizon of the human quest, is to be found within that quest, is the mystery by which the quest is borne along. It can be the quest for knowledge, the quest for choosing into history what is not yet, or the quest for love. Passion belongs to the quest: it urges one forward. One may say that passion is the driving force in human life of the one who is called "holy." Freedom belongs to the quest as well: it is the arena where "holy mystery" is truly encountered. And as for beauty, that neglected dimension of the mystery of God, it is the language which summons the heart to passion and freedom and God. To the extent that Joseph Campbell calls one to the place of the beautiful and awakens in one both passion and freedom, to that extent he may claim a theologian's interest, for there the knowledge and love of God are to be found.

NOTE

1. Walter Burghardt, *Tell the Next Generation: Homilies and Near Homilies* (New York/Ramsey: Paulist Press, 1980) 16.

CHAPTER SIX

The Campbell Phenomenon and the Uniqueness of Jesus Christ

Brian O. McDermott, S.J.

My purpose is to answer the following question: What would you, as a Roman Catholic systematic theologian, want to say to those reflective Christians who are both attracted to Joseph Campbell's approach to the world of mythology and, at the same time, upset or confused by his way of dealing with the issue of Jesus Christ's uniqueness and the uniqueness of the Christian story?

I respond positively to the invitation to address the question because I do not hear in it a summons to do the impossible. This whole arena of Christianity and its relationship to other world religions is in many respects so new, so immense, so challenging, and so controversial—indeed, at times, so numbing—that setting boundaries is very important.[1] One of my areas of research and teaching is Christology; actual dialogue with representatives of other world religions as such is not part of my life. Perhaps it should be. So I must acknowledge a need to be modest here. Dialogue is going on, in great depth, among representatives of the world religions, and with unforeseeable consequences, and such dialogue is necessarily influencing Christology in many ways. It raises not simply an "auxiliary question" in that field but rather a set of issues that underlie any Christology.

I will organize my reflections around four points: (1) Joseph Campbell and the Quest for Unity; (2) Mapping the Theological Terrain; (3) Holding Truths in Tension; (4) Praxis Precedes Theory.

Joseph Campbell and Quest for Unity

Joseph Campbell discerned a fundamental "monomyth" within and below the many patterns of religion and mythology in human history.[2] For Campbell the many can be reduced to the one, although he values the many ways in which the one is articulated. It is as if he is saying that deep down, all religions and mythologies are saying the same one thing, more or less, with greater or less success, with greater or less impact on particular peoples at particular times.

Robert Segal has very competently examined Campbell's work and finds that, when all is said and done, Campbell finds many similarities among the world's major mythologies, and considers these similarities more significant than any differences.[3] Moreover, Campbell is able to extract those similarities and express then in a uniform way that in a sense "transcends" the various particular instances of the myths. There is something very attractive about this, for are we not all seeking a uniting unity among the extraordinary variety of human experience in all its social, cultural, historical, and political diversity?

The cost of such a procedure can be immense, however. Absolved of all differences, the monomyth becomes an "absolute" that can turn anemic indeed.[4]

Campbell's appeal is powerful, however, because he touches the desire of people for direct relationship with the mystical within, immediate relationship with those sources of life and meaning from which institutions can estrange one. His invitation to humility as a dimension of the way always strikes a responsive chord. The ultimate reality that surrounds us and is within us is beyond our describing, but there is a path that can be described, or at least intimated, and this path can and must be lived out according to lights and symbols and rituals proper to particular cultures at particular times.

When committed Catholics read Campbell's treatment of the mysteries of Jesus' life, his birth, baptism by John, passion, death, resurrection, and ascension, they note how easily this scholar is able to move to comparable stories from other cultures and other parts of history. He not only—appropriately—challenges a literal reading of New Testament texts that are properly mythic in expression, but he seems to see an identity or equivalence of meaning present in these stories and in the stories drawn from other sources. For Christians who have never read the New Testament texts through a literary or historical-critical lens, what he says is at times shocking, but also salutary.[5] For better educated Christians, who have learned much from scripture scholars such as Raymond Brown or Reginald Fuller, the nativity narratives and the resurrection narratives cannot be reduced to general, schematically drawn parallels with other traditions, but rather are recognized as possessing a distinctiveness that cannot be shaved off or left behind for the sake of a premature unity or similarity.[6]

The question of Jesus Christ's uniqueness, a question that is posed to readers of Joseph Campbell, is not answered by him, nor is it the focal question of his work. Thus it will be necessary to move to the more theological terrain in order to do even minimal justice to this profound and extremely difficult topic.

Mapping the Theological Terrain

Recently, it has become customary to distinguish three basic positions regarding the question of the relationship between Christ and world religions. While this way of posing the alternatives can hide a great deal of complexity, there is enough truth in it to permit an initial "mapping" which is all that is possible here. These positions can be called exclusivist, inclusivist, and pluralist.[7]

According to the exclusivist position, Jesus Christ is the sole mediator of salvation and only those who explicitly believe in Christ will be saved. All other religions are mixtures of human good and evil but are not constituted by divine revelation. This position can refract into a subset of positions, depending on one's view of the role of the church. An exclusivist viewpoint prevailed in Catholic Christianity for most of its history. God desired all people to be saved, but the church was the necessary means of salvation. Catholic theologians admitted exceptions among those who did not belong to the church but who, having arrived at the age of reason, cooperated implicitly with grace, and in this way these theologians avoided an extreme form of exclusivism. But that extreme form is maintained today by fundamentalists of whatever denominational cast.

The inclusivist view contends that Jesus Christ is the unsurpassable revelation of God but that salvation from God is offered to all people regardless of their location in history or their explicit beliefs, provided they are true to the impulses of divine grace at work in their conscience. Those who hold this view will allow that God's revelation and grace is present in other religions in varying degrees, but that Christian revelation is needed to correct the error, or amplify the truth, of the other religion. The inclusivist position can maintain that God's revelation and salvation in Jesus Christ are both normative and constitutive for salvation, or simply normative. God's revelation and salvation in Jesus Christ are *constitutive* because the Christ-event provides the means of salvation for all people without which there would be no salvation in human history; other world religions are able to mediate the fullness of salvation because of the Christ-event and not because of a power or a truth that is expressed or rendered present in an ultimately reliable way by that religion. Revelation and salvation in Christ are *normative* because they offer the interpretive standard by which all other revelations and paths of salvation are to be evaluated: Christianity is the highest or purest form of revelation and salvation.

The documents of the Second Vatican Council represent this inclusivist position in its normative and constitutive form. In the "Declaration on the Relationship of the Church to Non-Christian Religions" (*Nostra Aetate*) the council reflected on the unity and common destiny of all people and spoke sympathetically and reverently of other religions insofar as they contain what is "good and holy" and reflect "a ray of that truth which enlightens all people."[8] Many theologians see an at least implicit affirmation in Vatican II that other religions can provide not only elements of revelation but a way of salvation for those who authentically live out the truth and love of that religion. A representative Roman Catholic theologian such as Karl Rahner would be interpreting Vatican II when he writes of the "anonymous Christian," a view that is widely known, and frequently criticized. "Anonymous Christian" was meant by Rahner as a term to be used among Christian theologians to indicate the conviction that God's grace communicated unsurpassably and universally in Jesus Christ is offered and active as justifying and sanctifying grace in the lives of all people. The phrase is tied to Rahner's understanding of the normative and constitutive role of Christ and of the role of the church in the salvation history of the human race.[9]

The official, inclusivist, position of the Roman Catholic Church, at least insofar as it comes to expression in Vatican II, is, to be sure, an enormous advance over previous church teaching. It gave an official endorsement of and encouragement for interreligious dialogue, a "wider ecumenism" beyond the religious colonialism and imperialism of the past. Vatican II's teaching put Catholic Christians in the position of entering into a dialogue in which they would not only offer occasions for transformation to others, but would themselves be led to recognize surprising ways in which God has dealt with those outside the church.

The teaching of Vatican II invites the church to inaugurate a third age in its development. If Karl Rahner is correct, Christianity, which was first Jewish-Christian and soon opened itself to Gentiles without their first needing to become Jews, is now entering a third era in which people around the world will not have to first become western in their thinking in order to become good Christians.[10] This period of the "world church," as Rahner called it, will be revolutionary indeed, and yet, from another point of view, it will be making good on some promising initiatives ventured by pioneers like the Jesuit Matteo Ricci (1552-1610) in China, when a similar effort was made to allow the Chinese to become Christians precisely as Chinese. We might be seeing a first reading in the liturgy from the Bhagavad Gita, and sacred texts of the east being used as revered sources of wisdom about the nature of grace and sin. Even more significantly, if Christians of the east need not become cultural westerners in order to be Christian, issues such as the uniqueness of Christ may be approached in a very different way than in the west. Perhaps it will not be the kind of question that arises from a truly non-western Christianity.

But this is speculation beyond the official, inclusivist position of the church. Even within Roman Catholicism this inclusivist view is not without its critics. For some theologians such a position as the official Catholic one seems to imply a still powerful, albeit more subtle, religious imperialism, the employment of one historically conditioned religious norm to evaluate in an absolute fashion other extremely different religious approaches.[11] How can one historical event or belief or set of events and beliefs be used to offer a final interpretation of other events or beliefs that are also thoroughly of history?

This brings us to what one can call the pluralist position. Such a position on the part of Christian theologians (such as John Hick, Wilfred Cantwell Smith, and Paul Knitter) tries to take seriously the historicity of all religious experience, symbols, and doctrines.[12] The ultimate ground of reality, the transcendent Mystery, is admitted to be one by most pluralists, but the historicity and particularity of all mediations to that ground or Mystery are judged to be inherently partial, incomplete, and they become downright misleading or idolatrous if mistaken for the ultimate reality. Pluralists will admit that for Christians Jesus Christ is the unsurpassable communication of the transcendent Mystery, and that such is the Christian experience. They do not want to deny that experience. Some pluralists stress the particularity of the Christian experience, and do not consider salvation in Jesus either constitutive or normative for people of other world religions; the Christ event, insofar as it is true, will have relevance for other than Christians, but it will not be a normative relevance.[13] Other pluralists, such as Paul Knitter, believe that the question of the normative status of Christianity is an open one, to be answered only in the process of genuine, mutual dialogue.[14] Pluralists will sometimes say that they eschew relativism but embrace the relativity of the various traditions. But all pluralists seem to agree that the uniqueness of a religious tradition (uniqueness in the sense of its being the sole, ultimate source of salvation) cannot be decided in an a priori way, that is, prior to the encounter with other world religions.

Often pluralists will seek a theocentric point of view, which means that they find unity at the level of the transcendent ground or ultimate Mystery. Sometimes it appears as though the pluralist believes that there is a single way of speaking about that transcendent ground or ultimate Mystery that encompasses all the world religions, and that prescinds from the particular, historical paths. Yet even language like God, transcendent ground, ultimate Mystery, emptiness, nirvana, non-self, or whatever is used to refer to the primal reality, is language that emerges from particular paths and perhaps can never be separated from those paths. We have to be supremely cautious when trying to find equivalents in various religions: Buddhist *sunyata* and Christian *kenosis*, for example. Recent attempts to find convergence here are instructive and can be taken as representative of this sort of effort at dialogue and mutual understanding.[15] The task is incredibly difficult, it would seem, if you try to be resolutely faithful to the meanings of terms and kinds of experiences denoted in the respective traditions.

Pluralism is in many ways a threatening approach for mainstream Christians, both Catholic and Protestant. Certainly the voices which speak for it are minority ones among Protestants and Catholics. But there is more than threat here; there is very significant challenge. The move from exclusivism to inclusivism was a very difficult passage, and, at least for Catholics, never involved a transition from a pure exclusivism to a pure inclusivism. I cannot imagine Roman Catholicism adopting an outright pluralist position. Such a position seems to carry too many inherent difficulties.

To mention just a few of the difficulties: (1) at least in a western perspective, truth is not provincial, but possesses a universal relevance; (2) the revelation of God in Jesus Christ offers Christians a perspective on ultimate reality that is precisely their contribution to dialogue; (3) the notion of religious pluralism as proposed by western theologians is a construction of modern western liberalism and thus as particular as any other view; (4) there must be some standards by which any world religion can be judged. If finding the standard on the ultimate "level" is still too difficult for us, then at least there must be some standard drawn from the dignity of the human person; the authentically religious must be discernible from the demonic in a transcultural way.[16] All religions and religious phenomena are not equal or equally good; Christianity and all other religions as concrete, historical realities have manifested at various times behavior that is a perversion of their own truth and value.

Holding in Tension Several Truths

Christians are those religious people who offer Jesus Christ the absolute faith, love, and hope that should be offered to the invisible God alone, and who experience in Jesus Christ the salvation from sin that comes only from the living God. These two principles—the principle of worship and principle of salvation—flow from fundamental experiences at the beginnings of Christianity and eventuated in the first general councils (Nicea I and Chalcedon).[17] These principles continue to express the fundamental religious experience of Christians today. Christians experienced and experience the human Jesus, the crucified and risen One, as being for them and doing for them as only God can be and do for them. Moreover, they experience themselves as summoned to respond to him as one responds to God alone and in that response of worship and discipleship discover that, rather than engaging in idolatry, they are living human life as authentically as possible.

It is, therefore, fundamental to Christianity that Jesus Christ be worshiped and followed as the Way to the invisible God whom Jesus called Abba, and to do so in the power of the Holy Spirit. Christians experience God as given to them in a twofold gift, as outer word of truth (Jesus Christ) and inner word of love (Holy Spirit). Certainly Christians can recognize on the basis of the founding experiences of Christianity and the ongoing living tradition into which successive generations of Christians are engrafted, that Jesus Christ, as human, finite, relative, historical, is surpassable in many respects, as well as unique and unrepeatable. This very particular human reality which as such is not divine is, however, the real-symbol of the inexhaustible God.[18] On the other hand, this particular, relative, and finite historical reality is conjoined to the inexhaustible divine reality in personal unity. In the experience of Jesus Christ, the absolute, the divine, the transcendent, is manifested in and by the relative and historical yet not confused with it, and the relative and historical is not solely relative and historical because it participates in the absolute, the divine, the transcendent.

Is it possible in this time of globalization for Christians to hold firm to their own experience of Jesus Christ as possessing an absoluteness and relativity and relate to other religious symbols, narratives, and beliefs in an open way? That is, can Christians approach other traditions in a way that does not declare the other ways necessarily false because not Christian, or as ways that must be integrated into the Christian story in order to be "truly true," but rather ways that in their own fashion involve absoluteness and relativity?

In posing the issue this way, I do not want too simply to say that the mediations of ultimate reality are only or purely "relative" and "finite" and that the transcendent ground or ultimate reality is "purely" other than the mediations. Christians cannot say that. I suspect that, from their own perspectives, believers in other traditions cannot do so either, especially given that their awareness of sameness and otherness is more supple than the usual westerner's awareness. Christians believe that Jesus Christ is relevant, indeed absolutely significant and saving for all history: Christianity is a world religion. Buddhist and Hindus contend that their experience is relevant and supremely significant for all people as well: theirs are world religions as well. There is a universality about each of the major religious traditions.

For me one of the most promising developments in what can be a bewildering thicket of possibilities is that new phase that the church is entering: the period of the World Church. For here praxis is outdistancing theological theory.

Praxis Precedes Theory

As a systematic theologian who has had his thinking shaped by the experience of Vatican II and theologians such as Karl Rahner, I have come to see that the council, and the theologians who both shaped it and remained faithful to its inspiration in the time that followed the Council, are way stations, profoundly significant way stations on the journey of the Catholic Christian people. But there is a form of Christian praxis (that is, spiritually and intellectually informed activity that intends the transformation of history) occurring in our world at the present time that holds together these several truths at the same time, even when there is no generally agreed upon theology underpinning the praxis. I am referring to figures like Bede Griffiths and Raimundo Pannikkar in India, and William Johnston and Henri Dumoulin in Japan (to name only a few).[19]

These Christian pioneers of the spirit in India and Japan have been doing something that would seem impossible: precisely as

Christians they have been entering deeply into Buddhism and Hinduism, passing over to the other standpoint, to use John Dunne's expression, and returning to their own Christianity, and finding in that adventure of the spirit more than a growing toleration of another religion, but an openness to its truth and love and an enrichment of their Christianity.[20] Now this enrichment does not come about by simply borrowing from these other religions. There is certainly no sense that these Christians are simply "dipping" into this other faith. What is going on? I do not feel equipped to describe, much less explain, the process that they are undergoing, but it seems safe to say that they are at the very least learning how to hold on to two truths simultaneously, the truth of Christianity and the truth of the other tradition experientially entered into. These two experiential truths do not come to a conceptual or even experiential "higher unity" in themselves. Yet these pioneers cannot deny either truth, nor understand one truth as negating the other.

Everything in a Western Christian might rebel at the prospect of a religious person deeply committed to his or her understanding of ultimate reality and to the mediator of that reality simultaneously passing over into the experiential realm of another religion and letting the experience occur without judgment, but rather with gratitude. Some people will want to protest: "Surely critical thought should be able to locate these two `experiences' in relation to one another, and to determine which is the more universal truth which includes the other, less universal one, granting that both are authentic." But are not these pioneers of the spirit, who kneel on the boundary between two world religions and who are willing to cross over the boundary so as to return with new experience and new understanding, offering a new paradigm to Christians, one that has the potentiality of profoundly influencing our traditional ways of thinking about other religions? Their praxis suggests to some that the concept of the uniqueness of Christ might properly be considered a product of western discursive thought and possessing a compelling claim on the mind only to the extent that one absolutizes the western mind-set. Perhaps a deeper question raised by these pioneers of the spirit is: Why is the question of uniqueness so important, so central an issue? The question may well be a culture-bound one.

The pioneers I am referring to, who remain followers of Christ as the Way and who pass over into another tradition not simply through interreligious dialogue or theological reflection but by the way of religious experience, are neither religious pluralists nor religious monists in their way of proceeding. Some other kind of logic is involved here. Would it be correct to surmise that they pass over into the other tradition with the expectation that the other tradition in its truth will not contradict the essential content of Christian revelation, but neither will it simply complement or enrich that revelation either? Do they not acknowledge that the experience of the Buddhist, Hindu, and Christian are different experiences, not simply the at-root same experience interpreted differently?

This is where Campbell's notion of the monomyth is misleading. His hunger for unity and universality seemed so great that he was not able to do justice to diversity. If it is true that there is no single, ultimate religious experience that unites all peoples of all times and places, then surely there is no single basic narrative that unites people either. The differences are as important as the commonality, but even this statement of the state of affairs is not definitive.

Catholic and other Christian theologians are not at all united about the relation of Jesus Christ to the world religions. In the history of Christianity the issue is an old one, but the amount of data and the quality of encounter between the world religions in the past never matched what is available to thinking Christians in our time. From this perspective the issue is very, very recent. We are invited to an immense amount of patience, of sifting out relevant data and paying reverent attention to it, of coming to understandings that do justice to the data, and undergoing the moral conversions and increasing religious conversions that allow us to live without a kind of clarity and certitude that Christians used to enjoy. Things are much more complicated now, but not because theologians have a penchant for always making the simple complicated (but that does happen all too often!) but because Christianity is learning anew from a critical and religiously converted reading of the New Testament that Jesus of Nazareth, living, thinking, and acting in a particular time and place in history, was bent on breaking, in the name of his God and the Good News he came to preach, all manner of boundaries about insiders and outsiders, about what constitutes purity and impurity, about who was included in salvation and who not.[21]

As Christians move from a Christological and soteriological exclusivism to a theocentric and Christological inclusivism in their thinking in the spirit of Vatican II, shared life and thought and prayer among representatives of the world religions continues, and holding onto both the saving truth of Jesus Christ as relevant not only for Christians but for all people, and the possibility that saving truth and love are offered in other historically and culturally mediated ways seems to be the stance that we are called to take up. It will not be a comfortable stance; but morally and religiously converted people recognize that comfort, absence of tension, is not a sign of either truth or goodness.[22] For some, pioneers of the spirit and theologians who seek to reflect "on the boundary," the tensions are part of the journey. Perhaps the experience of a student of mine at Weston School of Theology will become more and more common, and more and more the food of theologians' thinking. This man lived as a layman in Japan for six years after a number of years as a Trappist monk in the United States, where he prayed the Jesus Prayer and was schooled by the *Philokalia*. As a Catholic he has seriously studied Zen for many years. At a crucial time of his life he had the following experience:

> One day as I was standing on an old bridge in Japan's ancient capital of Kyoto, I heard the beating of my heart. Upon hearing it, it was as if I had never heard it before. I, for lack of a better word, died in that instant. Then, the Prayer of the Heart showed its face. Brightness in every direction. Shops and trees, youth and age, life and death. "Jesus," simply "Jesus." No realization of oneness, however deep and expansive, nor experience of otherness, regardless of how transcendent in Mystery, could survive this "Jesus." "Jesus," pure and simple. In this way I say: Not one, not the other.

> It was on this day that I realized I was a Christian. But not Christian as opposed to Buddhist. Just Christian. Jesus as opposed to the Buddha did not save me. Neither did a Jesus diluted to include all salvation figures save me. Nor was it a salvation which occurs irrespective of the particular savior. Neither coming from, to, or within: Salvation. Not one, not other.[23]

Would Joseph Campbell, the former Roman Catholic, and this Roman Catholic who experiences the truth of his religion in this fashion on this bridge in Kyoto, be able to understand each other? I think they would.

NOTES

1. For a comprehensive review of the current state of discussion, see Paul F. Knitter, *No Other Name? A Critical Survey of Christian Attitudes toward the World Religions* (Maryknoll, NY: Orbis, 1986).

2. Robert A. Segal, *Joseph Campbell: An Introduction*, rev. ed. (New York: Mentor, 1990) 32.

3. Ibid. chapter 9.

4. This is one of the principal concerns of Segal.

5. For an overview of modern New Testament scholarship, see John S. Kselman and Ronald D. Witherup, "Modern New Testament Scholarship," in Raymond F. Brown, Joseph A. Fitzmyer, and Roland E. Murphy, eds., *The New Jerome Commentary* (Englewood Clifts, NJ: Prentice-Hall, 1990) 1130-1145.

6. See, for example, Raymond F. Brown, *The Birth of the Messiah: A Commentary on the Infancy Narratives in Matthew and Luke* (Garden City, NJ: Doubleday, 1977); Reginald H. Fuller, *The Formation of the Resurrection Narratives* (New York: Macmillan, 1977).

7. See the helpful survey by J. Peter Schineller, "Christ and the Church: A Spectrum of Views," *Theological Studies* 36 (1976) 545-556.

8. "Declaration on the Relation of the Church to Non-Christian Religions" (*Nostra Aetate*) in Austin Flannery, ed., *Vatican II: The Conciliar and Post Conciliar Documents* (Northport, NY: Costello, 1988) n. 2, p. 739.

9. Karl Rahner, "Anonymous Christians," *Theological Investigations* VI, trans. K.-H. and B. Kruger (New York: Seabury, 1974) 390-398.

10. Karl Rahner, "Basic Theological Interpretation of the Second Vatican Council," *Theological Investigations* XX, trans. E. Quinn (New York: Crossroad, 1981) 77-89.

11. For these criticisms, see Knitter, *No Other Name?* chapter 8.

12. Ibid.

13. Ibid.

14. Ibid. chapter 10.

15. See, for example, the essays by Maseo Abe and the responses to them by a number of theologians in John B. Cobb and Christopher Ives, eds., *The Emptying God: A Buddhist, Jewish, and Christian Conversation* (Maryknoll, NY: Orbis, 1990).

16. Langdon Gilkey, "Plurality and Its Theological Implications," in John Hick and Paul F. Knitter, eds., *The Myth of Christian Uniqueness: Toward a Pluralistic Theology of Religions* (Maryknoll, NY: Orbis, 1987) 37-50.

17. Tad Dunne, *Lonergan and Spirituality: Toward a Spiritual Integration* (Chicago: Loyola University Press, 1985) 130-132.

18. Karl Rahner, "Theology of the Symbol," *Theological Investigations* IV, trans. K. Smyth (New York: Seabury, 1974) 235-240.

19. Bede Griffiths, *Return to the Center* (Springfield, IL: Templegate, 1977); Raimundo Panikkar, *Intrareligious Dialogue* (New York: Paulist Press, 1978); Heinrich Dumoulin, *Christianity Meets Buddhism* (La Salle, IL: Open Court, 1974); William Johnston, *The Still Point: Reflections on Zen and Christian Mysticism* (New York: Harper and Row, 1970).

20. John S. Dunne, *The Way of All the Earth: Experiments in Truth and Religion* (New York: Macmillan, 1972).

21. John Riches, *Jesus and the Transformation of Judaism* (New York: Seabury, 1982) 100.

22. Dunne, *Lonergan and Spirituality* 65.

23. My thanks to Mr. David Duncavage for permission to quote him.

CHAPTER SEVEN

Joseph Campbell's Spiritual Challenge

David Steindl-Rast, O.S.B.

The second, third, and fourth chapters of this book deal with the works and person of Joseph Campbell from a philosophical point of view. The next two approach the subject from a theological perspective. I am addressing Joseph Campbell from the spiritual point of view.

What do we mean by spirituality? We must be sure we understand that. We all know that spirit means life breath. One way of translating spirituality, therefore, is simply to call it "aliveness," or if you want, "super aliveness." This is certainly something that Joseph Campbell stood for. This "aliveness" is something that he radiated. We know from our own experience that there are degrees to aliveness. Sometimes we are less alive than at other times. Maybe at one moment it takes a little more effort to be alive than at another. At any rate, we know that a person who is *really* alive is alive in many different areas of their being. Joseph Campbell was one of those persons who was alive in many different ways. That is why just his personal presence was a challenge to our own aliveness. Joseph Campbell was a challenge to the spirituality, the aliveness, the super aliveness of all those he met. In his writing he was less interested in the meaning of life, than in the *experience of living*, in the experience of aliveness. I don't mean to say that he wasn't interested in the meaning of life, but that he was concerned with the meaning of life in an active way, a dynamic way. His challenge to all of us is to find life, to live life and not just to try to define it.

Rather than starting with Joseph Campbell as a challenge to our spirituality, I would like to start with ourselves, with our own experience. I would like to find a single starting point from which we can proceed, so I will try this. Here is the first paragraph of a letter written last Easter Sunday by a Quaker woman who the week before, during Holy Week, had a mastectomy, and who, on Easter Sunday went with two Catholic friends of hers to a Catholic church for the first time.

Easter Sunday, March 31, 1991

Dear David:

This morning with Markie and David, I attended Mass at St. William's. Though I felt a bit weak and wobbly, I was glad I went. I even intended to participate in the eucharist until the priest went so far as to announce that non-Catholics would not be welcome at the table.

I invite you to reflect on how this letter makes you feel. Focus on your feelings for a moment. Isn't it true that part of what you experience is a feeling of being torn apart. Suppose you were at that Easter liturgy and that you really enjoyed it, yet at the same time you were conscious of the plight of the woman excluded from the eucharist. How often we are torn apart in this way: half of us feels at home in the church, the other half totally alienated by the Church's actions. I would like to focus on this particular experience because, in my opinion, this is the area where Joseph Campbell brings the most pointed challenge to our spirituality.

A friend of mine once said to me, "My yearning for wholeness draws me to Joseph Campbell." I would like to discuss for a moment this yearning for wholeness, the challenge to our spirituality that Joseph Campbell presents, and the help that he can give us in finding wholeness. It is my contention that we are attracted to Joseph Campbell, in large part, because somehow we have a sense that he has a key to that wholeness which is the one thing we most lack. This touches the very core of our spirituality because our spiritual quest could be understood as our quest for wholeness. If aliveness is anything, it is wholeness. And that is what we lack. We are, in a sense, spiritually schizophrenic. Schizophrenia means, literally, a split mind. If we examine our feelings, many of us have a split mind especially with regard to our particular religious tradition. That is a great problem, and Joseph Campbell challenges persons with a split-minded spirituality to find wholeness.

I'd like to go one step further in exploring this split-mindedness. I suppose that some people might be familiar with Gregory Bateson's analysis of the origin of schizophrenia. Gregory Bateson had a very interesting theory, widely accepted by psychiatrists. He outlined the typical childhood setting, the family setting, the social setting of a child in which schizophrenia is likely to occur. He presented what is called the double-bind theory for the origin of schizophrenia, and it has four points. If the following four points are verified, the danger of schizophrenia is present.

First, there is present a deep bonding of the child with a significant other, normally the mother. Between the child and the other there must exist a sense of belonging, a sense of unity.

Second, the child gets double messages from the significant other. That is the decisive point. For example, the mother might say in a scolding manner, "You *know* that I love you." Or someone shouts at the other: "So, relax, I told you, relax!" Those are double messages. In the classic situation the child receives these double messages day after day after day in many different ways.

Third, the child has no way of clarifying the resulting confusion. For this third condition to be verified, there can be no point of clarification possible for the child, either because the child doesn't have the psychological distance to ask for it, or because the child doesn't have enough reflexive power. Even if the other three points are present, if the child in question has a way of saying something like, "Now, wait a moment, you say one thing and yet you act differently—why is this?", the danger of schizophrenia developing is not present.

Fourth, the child can't get out of the situation. That is where he or she believes they belong; a strong bonding is there.

Now, look at your own situation with regard to Mother Church. There is probably a deep bonding present between you and the church. If you don't have this bonding, the danger of being made schizophrenic is minimized. I have that deep bonding and I know that many others have it. I have this deep sense of belonging that I would never do anything in the world to break. I am an *Austrian* Catholic after all; and many reading this are *Irish* Catholics. Nothing is going to get us out of that!

Now notice the double messages you receive. Mother Church says "Shape up or ship out." She behaves in a manner that fits the worst stereotype of the father that insists on law and order, or imposes his will on the home. Think of the eucharistic table. "If you want to eat at this table, you will do this and this." Mother Church is absolutely insistent. And cold. Now, my father wasn't like that and I hope your father wasn't like that. What we see here is not the father; it's the stereotype of the bad father. It would be a terrible mistake to apply this stereotype to the biblical father that Jesus speaks of. Here is the double message we get: we relate to the church as "Mother," as one who is always there for you to return to no matter what you did, no matter how you messed up your life. Your mother will always embrace you and accept you. But our "Mother Church" sometimes acts like the stereotype of the bad father. There's the double message: a mother's reliable love and a cold demand for law and order.

Now the second element to notice is that you cannot question this situation, you cannot clarify this confusion because the one thing that you must *not* do is to question *the* authority of the church. Part of the bad father stereotype says: "Don't you dare question what I say in this house." The only way out of the tension would be to leave the household, leave the church. Some people have done it; some have tried to and failed. Leaving the church externally doesn't necessarily mean one has left internally. But if you can manage to leave, then you have minimized your chances of developing spiritual schizophrenia. You have, however, paid a very, very high price; it is a price that I personally would not feel willing to pay.

There is, fortunately, another way of getting out; that is to question authority. Here Joseph Campbell can be helpful to us. We can and we must question authority. We should do it, however, out of that deep sense of belonging to the church, which is something very positive, something you should want to cultivate, something that I personally, totally affirm. But out of a sense of love and care for the church we should question authority; we should do it respectfully, but clearly and firmly.

Religiousness Anchored in a Sense of Belonging

Now, how can Joseph Campbell be helpful to us in this area? The first point I would mention is that Joseph Campbell anchors religiousness in this very sense of belonging. In one of his interviews with Bill Moyers he was asked about his religious experience, and Campbell proceeded to speak about an experience of a sunset. Many will remember that wonderful scene where he speaks about the sunset, about his peak experience. That type of peak experience, whether it's a sunset or anything else, Campbell says, is the wellspring of our religious life. This is such an important point I suggest you pause for a moment and recollect one of those moments you have had that are beyond words, moments when one simply says, "Oh!" or "Ah!"

The great psychiatrist Abraham Maslow in describing this type of experience introduced the term "peak experience" into psychology. It is a very good and descriptive term. It describes a peak of our aliveness, a peak of our awareness. Maslow at first called them "mystic experiences" because they are indistinguishable on all counts from the religious experiences described by the mystics, but that name did not sit very well in psychological literature so he changed it to "peak experience." They are usually very short, but they are an elevated experience, a moment of vision, such as when you are up on a mountain peak.

Maslow observed that psychologists had spent decades exploring why people were sick and not fully alive. He asked the question: Why don't we look at those who are really alive and find out why they are so alive. The first thing that got his attention were these peak experiences. Eventually he came to see that all people seem to have them to some extent. But what is most interesting is that those people who are particularly creative, or psychologically healthy, or particularly alive, as you would say in everyday language, those people allow the energy of their peak experiences to flow into every moment of their life. They acknowledge their peak experiences. They can say "yes" to them. Other people regard them as moments of temporary insanity or some such thing. Maslow suggests that these moments may be are our only sane moments.

Reflect now, for a moment, on a peak experience you have had. Many things can be said about each one of our peak experiences. But there is one element they all share: a sense of belonging. Most of the time we go around feeling as if we are orphans in this world. We feel like outsiders, not quite included. But, in a peak experience for at least a moment, you feel you really belong. First, you belong to yourself; you are no longer schizophrenic, but rather you are really "together." Second, you belong to all others, and not only to all other people but to all other plants or to whatever is around you—rocks, clouds, the sky. You experience a sense of deep unity, of limitless unity, which includes a unity with God, if you want to use that term—with the Ultimate, the horizon of everything, the source of reality. You belong in every respect. We could understand our whole religious quest as a quest for that sense of belonging. If you have that, you have ultimate bliss. That is where the bliss lies that Joseph Campbell talks about. In those moments, your peak moments, you know what that bliss is. And you can now follow your bliss. You have been given a taste of your bliss. At that peak moment you also have found your true identity; you have found your Self.

Raimundo Panikkar makes an important distinction between identity and identification. Your identification is what you show to the sheriff when he stops your car because you have been driving too fast. Your identity is what you discover in your peak moments. It is your true Self. Your identity cannot be expressed in "I am this" or "I am that." Whenever you say, "I am a teacher, I am carpenter, I am a fast driver," that is your identification. Your identity is expressed like this: "I live, no longer I, but Christ lives in me." Now, if you and I can say that along with St. Paul, then the Self of ourselves is one, you see. You have found that oneness, that wholeness, where we all hang together.

You have also found meaning in this peak moment, because meaning is that within which we can find rest. "Restless is our heart," said St. Augustine, "until it rests in you, O Lord." Augustine pointed to God as being the source of all meaning. Not the kind of meaning you look up in a dictionary, but ultimate meaning as in "it means something to me." That is what you also have in your peak moments. You say, "That's it!" Adam said that when God brought Eve to him. "That's it!" You remember how God paraded all the various animals before Adam and he named each one. Naming in the Bible means "I've got your number." But then God brought woman before him, and Adam thought, "I'll never get her number." The mystery. That was a peak experience for Adam. He was confronted with the *great mystery*. We also have that experience in our peak moments.

Distinguishing Religiousness from Religion

The second helpful point in Campbell's thinking is that he distinguishes between religiousness and religion. Now he does not, to my knowledge, use the term "religiousness" and he is not particularly careful in his use of the term "religion" either. We all have our shortcomings and Campbell was not particularly careful sometimes in the way he talked. But nevertheless in his aliveness Campbell radiated religiousness, which he clearly distinguished from the religions of the world. We must admit that Campbell was a great religious thinker. Religiousness for him was anchored in what he calls the "common message." The common message of the myths. He is referring to those peak moments, those encounters with deep meaning. Since Campbell clearly distinguished religiousness from the religions, you may well ask how on earth does one get from that mystical religiousness to all those religions? How does one get from one to the other? My answer is a one-word answer. Do you know how you get there? *Inevitably.*

That word "inevitably" has all sorts of overtones and undertones, you see. But, at any rate, there is no way of *not* getting there, of not getting from religiousness to religion.

Let me demonstrate this from your own experience. Please try to follow me from within. People are different when it comes to the type of religious experiences they have. Some people have "big bang" peak experiences. Others never have those. Some have a slowly growing awareness, like a ground swell. What counts is not the shape of the experience but that deep sense of belonging. Now the moment you have this elevated, mystic awareness your intellect inevitably tries to understand it. Our intellect is built in such a way that we have to try to understand ourselves. Our intellect tries to interpret what happened. And the moment you have the simplest interpretation of what happened, you have the start of one of the most important elements of religion—doctrine. That is how doctrine comes about, by the intellect interpreting religious experience, the mystical experience. Even if your intellect says "that experience cannot be put into words, cannot be interpreted, it is totally ineffable," that is a doctrinal statement. We call it negative theology. So, you cannot get away from doctrine. Inevitably you go from mystic experience to doctrine. Doctrine is one key element of religion.

Another is morality. Not only your intellect, but your whole person, your whole heart responds to the peak experience. You begin to say we should all relate to one another as if we really belonged to one another. Christ really lives in me and in everyone else. Love your neighbor because you and your neighbor are really one. You say, "Wow, this is the way one ought to live—like one belongs." "This is also how we should relate to animals and plants, to the cosmos and to our environment." Everything is related in the peak experience moment. And that is the beginning of morality. Morality is nothing but an explication of how one relates and acts when one belongs. That is what ties all the different moralities in the world together. They may look very different and indeed they are in terms of their cultural setting and language and so forth, but they all have one thing in common: they express how one should act when one belongs. The different moralities of the world never contradict one another. Some do not go as far as others. Some draw the circle of belonging smaller than do others, but they all have that one thing in common.

The third equally important element of religion is celebration. You cannot help but celebrate this experience in some way or other. That leads you to your own private ritual. Ritual is the celebration of the mystic experience. You may celebrate it in a very subdued way if you're just talking about your personal religious experience. You may just say "Oh, every time I pass this bench in the park, my eyes light up and my heart gets light. That's where I had this wonderful experience, you see." So, what is that? That is remembrance, which is the essence of ritual. And it sometimes even entails a pilgrimage, because you make a little detour to go past that bench. Or you may remember a special day, say April 15, because that was the day you had a special experience. See, you already have a liturgical calendar. It's all in there. Inevitably, you see, we get to ritual celebration.

The fourth element of religion we want to consider is its communal and institutional nature. We have been talking about an experience of belonging. An experience of belonging is essentially an experience of community. With community comes institution. They are two very different things, but they are inseparable from one another. They differ in this way: institution has no heart, but community has a heart. You can say of a community: "All were of one heart and one mind," as we read in the Acts of the Apostles. Community and institution are inseparable because as soon as you have people together, even in the most rudimentary way, you have to institutionalize the group. In a religious community, what gets institutionalized is doctrine, morals, and ritual. Now what is the danger when an institution (without a heart) does that? The danger is that everything gets frozen. The danger is that what was like flowing water becomes as hard as ice. Now don't get me wrong; one cannot do away with institutions. But they are necessary evils, and I put emphasis on both those words. We might as well deal with them and deal with them lovingly. We cannot get away from the institutional aspects of the church, and the devil you know is better than the devil you don't know. But you are responsible for it, so you change it. It is necessary for life. Inevitably life creates structures, but structures do not create life. Therefore, we have to take those structures we live with and adjust them to our "aliveness." Joseph Campbell, for historical and biographical reasons, sounds even hostile, at times, when he speaks of religion. I believe it is because he rejects the frozen state that occurs in religions. His own religiousness was so pervasive in his life that he rejected anything that attempted to freeze it.

Personal Religious Experience

The third element in Campbell's thinking which is helpful to us is that he places great importance on personal experience, personal religious experience. Let me stress the word personal, not private. We do Campbell an injustice if we think he meant private experience when he means personal. They are opposites. What defines you as a person is precisely your relatedness to others. Personal means communal. Private would mean that you are cut off from others. There is no such thing as a private religious experience. Religious experience is an experience of belonging, of being related.

Now the function of religion, of its doctrine, its morals, and its rituals is to lead us back, again and again, to personal religious experience. What happens in religion is that, after some time, the doctrine which originally was simply a statement that reminded us of our religious experience and led us back to that experience because it was an interpretation of and a pointer to that experience, itself gets interpreted. Then the interpretation is interpreted and you wind up with interpretation upon interpretation. Ultimately it becomes very difficult to get back to the original experience through many layers of interpretation. Campbell emphasized, in his own way, the necessity of getting back to the original ground of this experience.

The same happens with moral teaching. At first moral teaching is simply a reminder that this is how one acts when one belongs. But then the teachings get engraved in stone and when situations change, the static laws become irrelevant. They cease to be reminders and become restrictions—a list of "do's" and "don'ts."

The same happens with ritual. You first do ritual to celebrate the religious experience you have had. Then gradually you forget what the experience was and you keep doing the ritual carefully, the way they used to do it. Finally the ritual is all rubrics (directions) and is no celebration of the experience. We have to push through continually to our own personal experience in order for ritual to function. Joseph Campbell emphasized that function of ritual very much.

Doctrine gives us a map, but it is not the journey. I am not rejecting doctrine. I am profoundly grateful for having been brought up in a tradition that has a strong doctrinal tradition and I am saddened when I see that so many young people have been brought up without it. That is a great loss for human life. But it is an equally great loss and burden to one's life if you have only doctrine and morality and rituals and no life. Doctrine gives us a map and for that we should be most grateful; but you must go on the journey for yourself. As you go on the journey, you may have to correct the map a little bit because you may see that the river has changed its course, or that it was not mapped out quite correctly. You might be the first one to see it correctly; why not?

To sum up so far, we have seen that Joseph Campbell anchors our religiousness in the sense of belonging; distinguishes that religiousness from religions; emphasizes the importance of personal experience. But because deadening rigidity is such a danger for religious institutions, he also challenges the authoritarianism of religion.

Religious Authoritarianism

Here is a pretty safe rule of thumb: When you are reading Campbell and you come across a passage that seems particularly critical of religion, it is in fact critical of religious authoritarianism. Now, how do you distinguish genuine authority from authoritarian authority? It is very important to make that distinction because obviously there is a place for valid authority. What does the word "authority" mean? Current dictionaries define the word to mean something like "the power to command." That is very far from the original meaning of authority. Originally authority meant a firm basis for knowing and acting. If a person is found to be a firm basis for knowing and acting, then that person is called an authority. If you are ill and you have to have an operation and you want to get a second opinion, you go to an authority in the field. An authority is someone who really knows the field and will be a firm basis for knowing what one should do in such a situation. Certain persons in a family, or in a neighborhood are known for being a firm basis for knowing and acting. Because of this they have, to some extent, a certain power to command.

Now once a person has gotten power to command, they will tend, unfortunately, to hang onto that power, even when they are no longer a firm basis for knowing and acting. When that happens, you have authoritarian authority. Authoritarian authority keeps itself in power by putting others down. Genuine authority's function is to build other persons up, to help them know and act. You can always tell the difference between these two kinds of authority by asking this simple question: Does it build me up or does it put me down?

Jesus caused a completely new understanding of authority to be spread through the world. I do not have time to develop this point fully, but let me give you just two pieces of evidence to support this claim. One thing that is absolutely certain about the historical Jesus is that he taught in parables. Parables were his typical method of teaching. The parable introduces a completely new concept of religious authority. Notice, first of all, that although Jesus was at one point called a prophet, that title did not stick to him. In not one passage in all the Gospels will you hear Jesus say, as the typical prophet would say: "Thus speaks the Lord." Jesus did not appeal to divine authority as the prophets did. Did he appeal to divine authority residing within him? The Gospel of John may give you the impression that he did but there is significant evidence in the synoptic Gospels which shows that Jesus did not typically say "I am the authority."

Where did Jesus place the divine authority on which he based his teaching? Listen carefully. In the hearts of his hearers. That was the unprecedented change. The parables demonstrate how Jesus did that. First, parables usually start out with a question such as, "Who of you does not know this?" The implied answer is that everybody knows that. It is common sense. Then comes the clincher. Jesus says, "Well, if you know that, why don't you act accordingly?" The joke is on the hearer. That is how a parable works. In using parables Jesus placed divine authority in the hearts of his hearers because he recognized that it was there. People said of Jesus, "This man speaks with authority." When are you moved to say that of another? When they stand there and claim they are the divine authority? Or when someone helps the divine authority within you rise up and hence builds you up?

Second, remember that at the Last Supper Jesus washed the feet of his disciples. Jesus told his friends that the authorities of the world put their subjects down. But with his disciples, it should be the opposite. The one who has the highest authority should be the servant of all. This is a complete turnaround of the notion of authority.

And this is ultimately why Jesus died on the cross. Jesus died because he built people up and he handed over to them the authority that was theirs. When that happened both religious and political authoritarians ganged up together and put him down. It happened then and it happens now. You only need to look at Central America and at some other parts of the world to see that it happens exactly as it happened to Jesus. Joseph Campbell challenges us to question authoritarianism.

Linking Spiritual Life with Myth and Archetypes

The fifth and final element in Campbell's thinking that I find helpful for us is that he links our spiritual life with myth and archetypes. Please return with me for a moment to my description of how we move from our peak experiences, our mystic experiences, to religion. We said that religious experience inevitably leads to doctrine, to morals and to ritual because your intellect, your will and your emotions respond to that experience. But there is a little moment, so to speak, before the experience gets translated and reflected upon this way, a little moment in which the mystic experience expresses itself first in myth and archetype. This expression comes before any of the key elements of religion develops. The myth actually contains the doctrine in story form; it also contains the morality and it contains even the ritual because the ritual is just the acting out of the myth. The myth is pre-religious, if you will; it is closer to the mystic experience than either doctrine, morals, ritual, or institution. Joseph Campbell saw that, and his work helps us link that religious experience to the archetype before it comes to this or that religious expression, or this or that religion. The myth, you see, is simply an archetype in narrative form. This explains why Campbell and Carl Jung are so closely related in their thinking.

Jesus puts us in touch with archetypes. Through his parables and sayings he evoked key archetypes in the hearts of his listeners. "Behold the lilies of the field . . . behold the birds of the air." Recall the image of the father in the parable of the prodigal son. Recall the eating and drinking events, the sharing, the giving, "This is my body, this is my blood." If we can live out these archetypes, we have wholeness. This is why Campbell anchors our religiousness in the sense of belonging, distinguishes religion from religiousness, emphasizes our personal (but not private) religious experience, challenges our authoritarianism, and now links our spiritual life with myth and archetype. By doing so he helps us recover that wholeness which we have lost and are always in danger of losing through our brokenness, through our split-mindedness.

Campbell's teaching is very closely aligned with John's Gospel in which Jesus' whole message is expressed this way: "I have come that they may have life and have it abundantly" (Jn 10:10). Jesus is also presented in that Gospel as praying to the Father that "they may be one, even as we are one" (Jn 17:11): wholeness. If I were to ask what is the key word in the prologue to the Gospel of John, probably most people would say "the word became flesh." That is not the key part of the prologue. The key sentence in the prologue is "Any who did accept him he empowered to become children of God." He gave to each person the power to become, through faith, what he is. That is what it is all about. That is the oneness for which we so yearn.

Once I was asked: "Do you think that Joseph Campbell really understood the Catholic tradition?" I thought for a moment and then said: "I would put it this way: he did not understand how deeply he really did understand it." I want to suggest that we can make up for his lack of understanding. We can take both his understanding and his misunderstanding and let them become for us a challenge to fulfill our yearning for wholeness. If that happens, then the message of Joseph Campbell will have fallen on fertile ground indeed and will have brought forth much fruit.

CHAPTER EIGHT

Celebrating the Holy in the Ordinary

Gertrud Mueller Nelson

Back in the days when life was simple and I was a young art student in Europe, I hitch-hiked through the Massif Central in France tracking the Romanesque abbeys which are famous in that countryside. I was particularly interested in the tympanum—the recessed half-circle area, over the main portals of the church. This study was in no way boring, for there, carved in stone, I could always be guaranteed a powerful and elaborate scene. This was the space reserved for a towering Christ, enthroned in majesty and reigning over the tumult of the Final Judgment Day. These imposing reliefs depicted the high point in a great drama.

I noted every detail: below the throne, avenging angels blow their trumpets to the four corners of the earth. And each soul, stricken with terror, scrambles forth from a grave to respond according to his or her own fate. Even in stone, the tension is electric, for each is to be weighed on the godly scales of justice. And as the shivering souls are weighed, a goat-like demon pulls down on the soul at his side of the scales, hoping to tip the balance in his favor and gain another candidate for his own fiery kingdom below.

Thus weighed, judged, and sorted out, the wicked damned are sent to the left hand of the Lord. And then these wretched souls— leave it to the French—are stuffed like so many vegetables into what looks like an early version of the Cuisineart: a gaping, toothy processor—the maw of hell, from whence they are spat out to a lower level, a hell of endless agony.

To the Lord's right hand, the blessed saved, reaching and crawling, shoving and pushing are herded, like the good sheep they are, to the doors of heaven—to be pulled up and now, finally, to rest in eternal bliss on the bosom of Abraham.

Left and right, good and bad, sheep and goats, heaven and hell, the great division is a graphic drama over the cathedral doors—a lesson carved in stone for all who enter here. The story seems to say that this Christ in majesty will finally reign over us all as fierce Judge and Ultimate Divider.

Certainly, the divinity over the church portal is a distant one— in no way do we meet here Emmanuel: God-with-us. This seems to be more a God-*against*-us. This is no picture of wholeness, of inclusivity, of all of us as one family. This is a Christ who reigns as final witness to our spiritual schizophrenia; that is, if he is not, indeed, the primary cause of all divisions. What is more, his final judgment will ultimately leave us split apart and divided from one another for all eternity.

As I went from one cathedral to the next, looking, drawing, making my notes, I'm sure that at least one time I followed the images down from the top, down from Christ's judgment seat, through heaven, through the tension between opposites that we come to know so concretely as the fate of our human condition. Then I followed the images through hell, and finally, much further down, dividing the great portals themselves; and at eye level I saw the Tree of Knowledge of Good and Evil with Adam and Eve at either side right here before me. They were in the process of making their fatal choice, *O felix culpa,* O happy fault, that "necessary sin" that brought about our great redemption.

Read in Reverse

Today, if I could go back to that spot I would read this scene differently. Personally and collectively we have been incited to new visions. I imagine that down here where any one of us stands eye to eye with Adam and Eve, I would reverse the way in which we have, over the ages, viewed that great and final moment.

What if we should simply read this story in stone, not from the top down, but from the bottom up? Then the very same image— read in reverse—leaves behind what we have always held as "a medieval world view" and becomes inspiration and instruction for our own time. Here, at the grassroots level the whole tympanum begins to take on a personal meaning. Here, where we place ourselves with Adam and Eve, we remember how each one of us was once simple and innocent. We were one with God—we walked with God.

One of my daughters, when she was about four, used to fashion banners out of whatever she could glue to the end of a pole. She called these her "precessions." "We need a precession," she would say, "so that God can come down and dance with us." And raising her banner into the wind, slowly, she would begin to dance. That's all it takes, when you are four—some scraps of cloth, a stick and tape, and God's your partner in a dance. In our innocence, God isn't distant. In innocence we dance with God and are equal partners.

The Human Condition

But we grow up and one day, like our archetypal parents, we too, are introduced to knowledge. We leave our simple, unquestioned, easy union with the divine and begin to ask questions. We sort and judge and choose. We choose this over that. We judge one thing to be good and the other bad. We learn right from wrong, up from down, left from right, male from female, joy from pain, life from death. And every division that we make calls for another division and another . . . Having once tasted this fruit of Knowledge of Good and Evil we develop a strong craving for more. And it is, indeed, knowledge which changes our easy relationship to God.

Our "fall" from innocence, as we have always called this moment, is the nature of the human condition. It is both archetypal and personal. It is our invitation to becoming human. It is the mixed blessing we enjoy: our freedom to choose together with the constant responsibility to pay a price for our every choice. Our "fall" is both the magnificent invitation to become human and our eternal temptation to forget that we are human, and "falling upwards" we think that we ourselves are God.

For isn't it here, in this second stage of our entry into the human condition that we begin to create our own heavens and make our own hells? Having chosen and having judged, we create those dynamics where one factor is ever in tension with the other. How often we tip the scales and lose our balance between left and right, active and passive, liberal and conservative, woman and man. As spouses and lovers, we get caught in wounding, futile arguments and can't quite understand how we got into this or how we'll get out. As neighbors we rage from opposite sides of the fence. Righteousness and rage are hurled, for instance, between those who are "pro-life" and those who are "pro-choice," each side lacerating the other with the fervor of moral rectitude. Individually, corporately, or internationally, one side wrests power from the other so that some become winners over the other who must lose. Between east and west, north and south, and between all of the religions "holy wars" are waged against "just wars." We despair that such factions will ever come to any accord. And, indeed, they cannot.

Between opposites, when both sides are right and both sides are wrong, we can only find the true answer, not in compromise, but in a third place. The answer is never either/or. It is both/and. It is over and above, in that sacred place which is larger than the sum of its parts.

But for that answer to emerge, a heroic gesture must first be made. Each side must abandon something of its own position to move with empathy toward the other, each gives up some of its power to approach the other in love.

Thanks to Campbell

We have Joseph Campbell to thank that he made popular and attainable for us the work of Eliade and Jung and Plato before him. Campbell's specialty and compelling gift was to show us, through the diverse mythologies and religions of the world, those core archetypes which we all have in common, that which connects us all at the deepest level.

It was, obviously, a heck of a revelation, or perhaps you wouldn't be reading this book, asking: so *now* what? Campbell infused us with fascinating material and returned to us the mythic and symbolic life. That was the fun part. But then Joseph Campbell skipped town to his Ultimate Bliss. And I'm here to tell you that everyone who knew him is now "a little bit pregnant." A little bit of knowledge is like that, and now we have to decide if we're going to carry this new responsibility to term.

For though many have sensed with a new relief that on some deep level we are all bound together as one, yet we are also different. What do we do with our differences? "East is east," the saying goes, and "west is west and never the twain shall meet." How, indeed, are we so different that our union seems only possible on the level of myth and archetype? For in a twinkling, it seemed, a marriage took place and before we fully realized it, Campbell's mysticism made gods and humanity, heaven and earth, spirit and body *identical*.

If Campbell's mythologies could turn us all back again to our Christian mythic heritage, we might rediscover a God so passionately in love with humankind that God had to become human, and remains human. In the marriage of heaven and earth, in the fleshtaking of the Spirit, in incarnation, indeed, the division of matter from spirit is obliterated and the two become equal and one. Furthermore, because of the mystery of the incarnation every level of reality is affected from the most basic molecules to the ultimate Being of God. This same passionate love of the divine is incarnate in each of us and imbues every ordinary thing with the sacred.

To believe in the mystery of the incarnation does indeed make this earth equal to heaven. And because of the incarnation, our ecological sensibilities and the Earth Movement, for example, find their urgency, their meaning and purpose. Every portion of the equation which is oppressed, poor, weak, literally underfoot or disenfranchised is the chosen partner in the mystery of the incarnation.

Difference

But it is also a part of our human process and our pain to know this difference and separation, which is possibly necessary in our experience, so that this marriage of opposites and the mystery of incarnation can take place in our human existence, over and over again.

Campbell didn't take up this second stage. He didn't concern himself so much with difference. He didn't show how the African story and the Chinese story were also different and are told differently.

I think that the feminist movement gets hung up repeatedly in the same way when we say, "Men and women are all the same! So treat us the same. It's easy!" So now women can change tires and men can change diapers! This hasn't seemed to resolve things much between us—because we only fiddled with superficial, cultural detail.

The feminine is not the *same* as the masculine, not identical. Though, thank God, we are finally getting the picture that these qualities belong to both men and women. What makes masculine and feminine values different? What makes them deeply, archetypally unique? Now, how can we give equal value to our differences so that in equality we may become partners and co-creators?

Neither are heaven and earth the same. But can we really come to believe and live as though they had equal value?

Matter and Spirit are not the same, matter is not a god—matter is the equal and worthy container of God. Without matter—*mater*—mother, God could not be known among us. But, we don't believe that, so we make of matter a god. We don't know the unique and holy property of matter and thinking it a god, we live lives of materialism. Consumerism is founded on the belief that we can buy the things that will save us. "All this I will give you if you will fall down and worship me."

God and humankind are not the same—we are not gods, rather we can be impregnated with God—can become worthy and holy conduits of the divine. As *equal partners in the dance, we become* one with God. And God is one with us.

Moses and the Burning Bush

A story of Moses comes to mind. I think of Moses, trotting along in the desert, doing a boring job. He herds his father-in-law's sheep, day after day in a featureless landscape. It's like driving the freeways, like paying the bills, like herding the children from the orthodontist to piano lessons. Always the same routine. Nothing new ever happens. One day, in herding his sheep, Moses sees a bush on the horizon. "Big deal," he might say. "A bush." And then trod on. Or perhaps he sees a fire? "Ah! A fire!" and he trods on. But Moses stops his routine. In stopping, in holding still, in looking, Moses allows the impossible to be possible. Opposites become superimposed. He recognizes that the ordinary green bush is imbued with the spirit-fire. Bush and fire do not cancel each other out. The bush is not burnt. The fire does not fizzle on greenwood. Rather, the seemingly impossible happens; the opposites become one thing to enhance and fulfill and redefine each other. And *because* he allows the impossible to be possible, Moses hears God call him by name, that is, he discovers who he is. He learns, right there, the meaning and purpose of his life and of his particular mission.

Annika and the Yam

God still speaks to us through the ordinary—if we will only stop and listen. I remember an occasion when my youngest daughter, having swiped all the half-grown potatoes from my garden, was using them for potato printing on the back patio. I was dashing about the kitchen preparing dinner for guests when I discovered I'd forgotten to buy asparagus for this meal. So I interrupted Annika at her work and asked if she'd please run down to the market and get me the asparagus. She agreed, washed up a bit, went to the store, and when she came she pushed the grocery bag across the counter to me, and with considerable solemnity said, "Mama, just look what I found at the market!" Now I was of a very efficient frame of mind and didn't really have understanding or patience for any surprises: "What do you mean, 'what else I found'? I only gave you enough money for asparagus and I hope you bought that." I reached into the bag and luckily I pulled out the asparagus. And then I reached in again and I pulled out a yam. One dusty yam. "What did you ever think I was going to do with a yam? A single yam! It doesn't go with the meal . . ." and on I fussed.

But the practical is always the enemy of the numinous. And Annika put her hand on my arm and said, "No, Mama, just look. Have you ever seen such a beautiful root? After all those tiny potatoes from the garden . . . this is a beauty." Why, her eyes shone. And for a moment I imagined this kid—this teenager with the baggy socks and the paint on her shirt-levitating amongst the produce! So I looked. And she said, "What is it? What's it called?" "Frankly, I don't really know the difference between a yam and a sweet potato," I had to admit. "What does it look like inside?" And so we took that dusty root to the cutting board and we sliced it and it fell open. Inside it was a beautiful burnt orange color. A whole sunset was caught in that root. She saw it and I saw it. We shared that experience. The humdrum and the numinous were all of a piece.

God still speaks to us from the burning bush, from the yam, if we can rise above our efficiency for a moment, if we can stop our routines. Then, when we stop and look, we hear God calling us from the burning bush, making us aware of our humanity and of the divine in what is so human. Elizabeth Barret Browning said: "Earth's crammed with heaven and every common bush afire with God."

The Symbolic Life

How will we live the symbolic life? Do we need to trot off and choose for ourselves a myth that strikes us? Do we go from one myth to the next picking up what attracts us?

Joseph Campbell himself wasn't able to live the Christian mythology he inherited, or so he led us to believe. A friend of mine, however, who was a classmate of his at the Jung Institute years ago told me that Campbell was an enthusiastic Catholic in those days and went daily to the eucharist, a practice which caused him to arrive late for lectures. Then he loved to rattle his friends as he entered and took his place by announcing in that booming voice we've all come to love, "I've just been to Mass," and he would beam, watching his classmates squirm out of embarrassment for him. *They* were enlightened: "When was Joe going to get over his projections on the church!"

Personally, I wish he hadn't "gotten over it," but had helped us all make the difficult transition into the new paradigm that the Second Vatican Council has invited us to do.

Jung himself, despite the fact that he found no collective container for his own religious sensibilities, gave us two bits of information that may be useful to us and which many people have never heard.

Jung felt that we may indeed need to look at the mythologies and religions of the rest of the world and know them and study them. He was fascinated with eastern religions. But he also indicated that we should know how they are *different* from our own and we should take most seriously the *archetypal mythology* into which we were born; there, where we drew our first breath, was the mythology that was ours. Certainly, to know and learn from and gain insight and disciplines from other religious systems will very likely turn us back to our own mysteries with a clearer vision that is enriched and illumined. It has done so for me.

Jung also said to a group of Anglican bishops back in the 1930s that the Roman Catholic Church had everything one needed for becoming a whole person if you really lived it's feasts and fasts, celebrated its dogmas, and participated in its sacramental and symbolic life. He told them that the trouble with them as Protestants was that they took dogmas and subjected them to "their playful intellects," which was only to render them unbelievable. It is no longer the 1930s and we Catholics have learned meanwhile to protest with the best of them, and have developed our own "playful intellects."

Dogmas

What now do we do with dogmas and doctrine? What do they really mean? I've come to believe that the word "dogma" means "that without which one cannot live." Not, "if you don't believe this you will go to hell." When something is right, we grab a mason jar, stuff the truth in it, hermetically seal it, and say, "Keep this." And then we forget what's in it. "Let us build three tabernacles and stay here at the peak experience forever." And Christ says, "not possible." What do we do with inside truth?

Let me offer another bit of wisdom which might prove useful at this point in our considerations. It comes not from Jung and it preceded Campbell's popularity. Unable to do much traveling to exotic lands once I had children, I took to playing anthropologist— at home. I learned to watch the rites and hear out the beliefs of three exotic primitives: my children. It was from the youngest I learned the following bit of wisdom.

When Annika was five, she underwent the standard tests that the public school required to find out if she was "ready for kindergarten." The psychologist had asked her:

> Annika, do your parents read to you?
> You mean, tell stories? she replied.
> Okay, tell stories. Do your parents tell you stories?
> Sure. My papa tells us Piggle-Wiggle stories and my mama tells us Greek myths.
> Really? Greek Myths?
> Ya, you know—mythology?
> Well, said the man, do *you* know what a myth is?
>   Would you like to tell me?
> She thought a moment. Well, a myth is a story that's
>   not true on the outside. But it is true on the inside.

Here, at the mid-level of our modern, human development, we are most often confused. We don't know the *difference* between inner truth and outer truth and think them *to be all the same*. We are tempted to see as false that which we cannot see. And not knowing the nature of the inner hunger that gnaws in us as a religious longing for purpose and meaning, we feed that inner hunger on the outside. We eat, we drink, we shop, we work with a religious compulsiveness. But the real religious hunger inside is not quieted.

Neurosis as Parody of Religion

Our neurosis is the modern parody of religion and is the consequence of our lost orientation to the sacred. Neurosis, habits, symptoms, and addictions rush in to fill the void left by our loss of religious practice and disciplines.

When we don't keep the holy fast, when we think ourselves beyond all that, then something else, something less conscious, takes its place. So today in our society we don't fast, but we are a whole society on diets, or breaking a diet, or determined to begin a diet. Thus, forever guilty about our eating, we have also lost the *joy of the feast*. Neurotic guilt keeps us from experiencing joy. The practices of the church aren't meant to make us feel guilty, or to put down our bodies. They are there to help us to live with passion and consciousness. We may need to fast *for* our bodies, and having fasted, we appreciate and rejoice in the feast.

When we refuse to "embrace the cross" in the constructive suffering that every life requires, we suffer neurotically—*all the time*. To "have a nice day" has become our constitutional right— ritual days of penance were once our official "bad days." Now we don't have a bad day. The bad day has us, whenever it wants. What good does it do for world peace, we say, that a few crazy masoch- ists fast on the Capitol steps? But their's is a right instinct. Because when we don't take inside—*into our own flesh* the suffering of the cross—as Jesus did it—the alternative is to play God, as Jesus did not. It is to inflict from our omnipotent distance unseen suffering on thousands of others. And all the while we complain of chronic low-back pain.

We project the inner darkness of our unconscious stirrings onto the darkness out there, onto the night, onto our dark-skinned sisters and brothers, onto everything that frightens us or that we don't understand, onto all that we can't see clearly, onto every- thing that is *different* from what we know.

We seek the inner truth out there and send out rockets to probe outer space, and wonder that we didn't find God there at a distance. That is to have forgotten that God's not out there, but rather God is God-with-us and seeks to be incarnate in the very flesh of our humanity. This realization returns us to earth with a new reverence.

It is always a temptation for us to believe that the everyday world and the sacred, the ordinary and the extraordinary, cannot meet. That conviction prevents us from having an experience of healing and wholeness. In fact, we cannot find our religious nature outside the setting of our human experience. The flesh-taking of the Spirit, the incarnation, is a mystery made new in our daily efforts to be fully human.

Rites and ceremonies, celebrations and liturgies are meant to heal that rift between the sacred and the everyday for us. They underscore our human experiences like loneliness and community, successes and failures, births, loves, lives and deaths. Celebrations encircle the transitional points in our lives, that is, those occasions when we risk moving another step forward into awareness and transformation. They act out our hopes for this kingdom and our belief in its goodness.

At their best, rituals are containers meant to hold safely for us something of the transcendent. I live near the ocean and when I take walks on the beach, I like to see the many ways people relate to the ocean and the powerful surf. Sometimes people come from a long way inland and seemingly they feel they have arrived at the edge of the world. They rush from their Winnebago, children in tow, and seem to announce, "This is the Pacific Ocean. That's all there's left between us and Japan." Sometimes they grab the smallest ones and without much preparation, dunk the little ones into this great, heaving water. Rarely is the baby thrilled with this almighty introduction. It's simply too much, and kicking and screaming they let you know.

One time, however, I watched a wise mother with her three children. They took their time. They stood well back from the surf and watched the rhythmic waves rise into great grey mountains, crest, curl, break, and whoosh up onto the beach only to be sucked back again into the next rising mountain of water. The ocean was powerful. And they stood in silence and watched. Then the oldest did something which perhaps all of us have done at some time. She turned her back on what was too much, and into the sand she began to scoop a hole. Into this hole she allowed something of the great uncontainable sea to whoosh up and be caught. Her brother then joined her and began to dig as well. Soon they had built a sizable hole, a containable sea, a mini-sea in which they could splash and jump and squeal. This was a sea she could handle. Then, suddenly a large wave came and wiped out one side of their hold, and shouting they hurried to rebuild the edges and fortify the sides. Another wave came and wiped them out again. And again they hurried to rebuild. Back and forth the children worked between what was containable and what was deliciously, frightenly uncontainable. For them, not only was the power of the ocean a religious experience, but the very act of relating to it was a religious experience. I see what the children did as a paradigm for our own need to make ritual: we make a container to catch safely something of the uncontainable.

A man told me recently, "I'm sorry, but I don't really need rituals because I'm never about to be blown away by a religious experience. In fact, I'd rather *like* to be knocked off my horse by a religious experience." I said, "Man, get a horse!" First we need a form out of which to be transformed. And the form, the system, the discipline needs to have sold walls so that it can indeed be a worthy container. Our problem is that we often also devise a lid for this container. That is, we think we can trap and keep the transcendent. But with that action we only seal out God or the taste of the transcendent. Each time we are confronted by a powerful experience, we need to come before the occasion with reverence. We need to name the moment for the religious experience that it is. And in times when we feel numb and like nothing touches us any more—like nothing could knock us off our horse—then it's time to go off and create the simple, earthly ritual that invites God to touch us. Go to the beach yourself. Roll up your pants legs and begin to dig. With suit coat and tie removed, we get down to earth and down to the business of creating a form in humility, in fear, in trembling, in the hope that we might be touched by God.

It is when we feel small, even insignificant and inadequate in our approach to the Holy Other—the One who is vast and uncontainable—that we use the elements of nature within our reach.

Nature and the things of this earth allow us to approach the untouchable through that part of God which we can touch. For this reason, the elements used in liturgy and religious celebration are so stunningly simple and familiar. It is the ordinary element that best becomes the container, the conduit or conductor for a safe touch of the Transcendent. These elements have sustained us for as long as history can remember and are always within reach. We encounter the transcendent in what is simple and familiar: in bread and wine, in fire and ashes, in earth and water and oil, in fasts and feasts, in pains and joys, in bodies and babies. Liturgy is not theology dressed up in the right vestments. It isn't heady ideas. It is up and doing in bodily action what the heart already knows.

It is the poetic church that nurtures us. It is this silent, mothering church, not a hierarchical church heard through the voices of men concerned with rules and exclusivity but this welcoming mother-church who has food for all who come to the table. With a smudge of ashes on our heads, with good dirt, she says, come friend, come on down to earth again. You are no god (and besides, you do a lousy imitation). Come, you are human and of this earth! And that matter is worthy. It is this matter—the stuff of your body—which is the worthy partner of the divine. And so also with waters, she washes us and names us. With oils she anoints us. In her ceremonies and rituals the experiences which make up our daily lives are affirmed and made sacred. And with all the sacraments and sacramentals she returns meaning and purpose to our lives and encourages us to feel and know and taste and smell and touch and live this human life with passion and awareness. For every transition we are compelled to make, she carries a blessing to help us cross the bridge safely.

My Kitchen

When I come home from jetting across this country, I can move so quickly and land in my kitchen so fast that I can re-enter in a state of dis-orientation before I've fully realized the transition I have made. I think I'm happy to be back. I think I'm pleased when I hug my husband and the kids. But then I survey the kitchen— which I think is my territory—and I discover to my irritation that they have used the kitchen in my absence. Promptly I fly into a cleaning frenzy, barking orders as I sweep and sponge and rinse. I have been taken over by an archetype, an imposter mother has replaced me. Then some clever child makes one parting shot as he disappears. She's riding her broom again. That's my unconscious ritual, and it makes for a clean kitchen, but it drives the family, one by one, to the farthest corners of the house.

I have also discovered that I can create a ritual that brings me down to earth again slowly. I can do it if I recognize my vulnerabilities in the dangers of the transition I am seeking to make. I remind myself that when I get home they will be waiting for me with stories and with questions, with feelings and needs of their own. I will greet them and focus on who they have become in the last few days. See them clearly. I will hear their stories, their successes and concerns. And we will chatter then, exchanging stories. And when they settle down, I too will have come down to earth again. Then I'll go into that kitchen, fill the dish pans with hot soapy water, and up to my elbows in suds, *artfully*, I will join in the work of the creator and behold, I will do my part *to make all things new*. Soap suds can do that. Getting down on all fours to scrub a bathroom will do it. Building a fire in the fire place, waxing the car, hanging clothes on the line, planting a garden—doing the earthy, ordinary task in an extraordinary way is to do the work of God.

Hopi Rite

Initiation into the sacramental life of the Christian mystery has some parallels in a Native American ceremony the Hopis perform with their children on the feast of the Kachinas.[1] They gather the young people in the great earthen Kiva as they have always done it, year after year. Down there, in the earthen womb, they await the dancing gods as they descend from the mountains beyond. They listen to hear the Kachinas approaching with their calling and singing. As the Kachinas draw nearer, the children call back, inviting them to enter through the hole at the top of the Kiva as they have always done it, year after year on this feast. They come to frighten the children with their masks, to tell their secret stories, to dance their dances and give their gifts and blessings to the children.

Then one day, when the children have become adolescents, they gather again in the womb-like Kiva and await the gods. Singing, chanting, bearing their gifts, the children hear the gods approach. They enter the Kiva and descend into their midst, but this time the Kachinas are not dressed in their special robes, nor are they wearing their special masks. The young people see for the first time that the Kachinas are their fathers and uncles and older brothers. Without explanation, the ceremony proceeds as it always has. Then the Kachinas ascend again and disperse.

The revelation shatters a naive faith. Dis-enchanted, the adolescents are wordlessly given a profound religious choice: they can either be distressed and disappointed at having been misled all these years, regret their lost innocence, and thrust away the

Kachinas as childish, or they can see this as an invitation into adulthood. They can understand from this ceremony that to be an adult in the community is to have been *impregnated* by that spirit and that to emerge from the Kiva now, is to return and to join the adult world in the godly work of the Kachinas. To carry their messages, tell their stories, and give their gifts is to make human and incarnational the work of the gods.

Thus, to be dis-enchanted is to recognize the difference between inside truth and outside truth, and *in the same moment* it is an invitation to be reconnected with our God impregnated with the divine. Our way back to a connection with God is actually a journey forward and through a profound experience of our humanity. When we live artfully the mysteries of our humanness, we will see beyond the obvious to the mysteries hidden in the ordinary.

Mandorla

We will bring about the marriage of opposites that brings forth the redeeming Christ when we live this human life imbued with the same passionate love that God has for us. For there—if we return now to the tympanum—crowning the whole story, at the very center and over and above the turbulent judgment drama, we now understand the Christ of majesty as the image of peace and equity.

He sits in the center of an almond shape called a mandorla, a halo that contains the image of the holy and the whole. This ellipse is the third form that occurs when two circles partially overlap.

Bring right and left together. Bring Spirit and matter to one place. Wed opposites and know God-with-us. Christ appears in that moment/space where left and right have merged. There he reveals a new truth, greater than the sum of oppositions.

Sometimes this Christ is depicted holding a book inscribed with an Alpha and an Omega, the first and last letters of the Greek alphabet: "I am the beginning *and* the end; I am both/and," it says. "Neither the first nor the last, but over and above both." "I stand", it says, "as that religious experience which is outside of time, which is the fullness of time, a vision into the eternal now." This is the place of peace.

In ancient illuminations where color was used, Christ is sometimes enthroned on a rainbow within this mandorla. Here where black and white meet, we do not just make grey compromises. Between black and white is every color of the spectrum. Wherever storm clouds and sunshine accept and enhance each other, wherever each knows and allows the other to be part of the truth, the rainbow appears for a few moments of utter beauty.

The vision this "last day" image portrays is not just a once and for all happening on some final calendar day; rather, it is a vision that appears in bits and glimpses whenever we give up our power struggles and reach out to the opposite side to overarch our differences—to create a rainbow of peace. In every marriage of opposites (and many of us know it so concretely in sacramental marriage) we can only meet and touch and create "a new heaven and a new earth" when we meet in empathy, when we approach the other— clear about who we are individually, emptied of our ego plots and pre-conceptions—but joined now where we are vulnerable. There we are willing to bear the other's burdens and share the other's joys—no grudging compromise here—trying to know to our very bones the fears and feelings that the other bears and to bring the other exactly what is needed. Come, inherit the kingdom prepared for you from the creation of the world. For I was hungry and you gave me food. I was thirsty and you gave me drink. I was a stranger and you welcomed me. I was ill and you comforted me, in prison and you came to visit me . . . As often as you did it for one of my least ones, you did it for me (Mt 25:34-36, 40).*

NOTE

1. This ceremony is described in John Shea, *Stories of God* (Chicago: Thomas More Press, 1975) 32-33.

* Portions of this paper appear in the author's *To Dance with God: Family Ritual and Community Celebration* (Mahwah, NJ: Paulist Press, 1986) and in her book *Here All Dwell Free: Stories to Heal the Wounded Feminine* (New York, Doubleday, 1991).

CHAPTER NINE

Is There a Christian Myth for Today's People?

Matthew Fox, O.P.

Is there a "Christian" myth for today's people? I'd like to say a few things clearly and directly by way of introduction. I put the word "Christian" in quotes for reasons that should be clear to anyone who understands what myth is. Thomas Aquinas refused to talk about "Christian" truth or "Christian" grace and this got him into a lot of trouble. (People forget Aquinas was condemned three times before he was canonized.) We run a grave risk in zeroing in too exclusively on anything called "Christian" myth. A myth that has power has it because it is true. When it is true it speaks to our insides, it arouses grace, it awakens the heart, the mind, and the soul that are asleep. It is an affront to Joseph Campbell's work to overemphasize the word "Christian" in speaking of "Christian" myth. In the celebrated television interviews with Bill Moyers, millions sat mesmerized listening to Campbell recount stories from Hindu myth, Islamic myth, and myths from many other cultures. The myths were true, and so they worked for us, at least to some extent. Campbell quotes the vedas saying, "Truth is one; the sages speak of it by many names." Thomas Aquinas in the thirteenth century said that every truth without exception and no matter who may utter it is from the Holy Spirit. He also said that the old pagan virtues were from God, and that revelation has been made to many pagans. Now having expressed this caveat about "Christian" myths, I will proceed to deal with them. These myths are big, big stories that are true and wise; they come to us through our Jewish and Christian traditions, through the Scriptures and through the mystics and prophets who have attempted to live out these Scriptures.

Is there a "Christian" myth for today's people? My answer is this: if there is not, if Christianity has lost its powerful story, then Christianity has no right to stick around as a religion. It is nothing but a lot of museums. Empty shells. Interesting past, but offering little for the future. A lot of empty shells: churches, seminaries, schools, that deliver empty heads, empty hearts, empty bodies, and empty souls. Empty, indeed, of power, and therefore, of spirit. The monk, Bede Griffith, once said to me: "If Christianity cannot recover its mystical tradition in a living fashion, then it has nothing to offer the world and it should simply close down." To talk of mysticism is, of course, to talk of myth. For myth and other art forms such as ritual, carry our deepest stories as individuals, and as a people. These stories are almost too big for words; they are too big for science alone, too big for the left hemisphere of the brain by itself.

My current definition of mysticism is awe. Mystical experiences are experiences of awe. After a lecture I delivered recently a very excited man approached me and said, "I am a brain researcher. For the last twenty-one years I have been doing nothing but research on the right hemisphere of the brain in a laboratory at Stanford University. I am now ready to publish my work. My conclusion is that the right hemisphere of the brain is all about awe. Now I have just listened to a theologian say that this awe is the heart of mysticism and that mysticism is the heart of religion. I'm shocked that you beat me to it." I replied, "We're not in competition; it's just that I come from an older tradition. Now we can team up." When science and mysticism get together, and if artists who can tell the mythic stories through dance, poetry, music, and ritual get aboard, the result is cosmology. When this happens, you have a renaissance; you have a true cultural awakening.

Certain elements of our civilization in the west, especially since the Enlightenment, have been busy destroying myth (just as we have been busy destroying rain forests, the aboriginal people of the rain forest, and their stories). We have attempted to sanitize this destructive effort by giving it a legitimate theological name called demythologization. The latest and silliest example of the effort to demythologize was reported in the Los Angeles Times a few weeks ago. According to a headline the Jesus Seminar, which is a group of very left brain, male biblical scholars declared: "Eighty percent of the words of Jesus in the New Testament and all the Jesus quotes in John's gospel are not really Jesus' words." Big deal! Have these people never heard of Christ? You see, the era of the quest for the historical Jesus has ended. And that statement is the last *reductio ad absurdum* of that movement. The quest for the historical Jesus which describes the last two hundred years of biblical scholarship framed a question that the writers of the Gospels never asked. They had seen the historical Jesus. They were interested in what Jesus meant. That's the Christ. This conference is important because it is a serious effort to put energy into re-mythologizing.

Otto Rank, one of the great prophets of our century, said fifty years ago: "Do not cure excessive rationalism with more rationalism." We have to step out of the demythologization consciousness: that is what Joseph Campbell did and that explains why he is so important for our time. He invited people to step out of that way of seeing the world and our sources, and invited us to start re-mythologizing. Saint Paul says that the letter kills, but the spirit gives life (2 Cor 3:6). Doctrine without myth or spirit kills. Spirit, after all, is about the infinite. Thomas Aquinas taught this amazing thing: one human mind is capable of knowing an infinite amount of knowledge. The proof he offered is that you never fill up your mind. On your death bed you can still be eager to learn another thing. Your mind is infinite. He also says your heart is infinite in its capacity to love, provided your mind is working to provide your heart with more lovable things. And, he also says that the human imagination, attached to its hands, can produce an infinite variety of artifacts. That is what it means to be spirit, to be spiritual. And this is why we need myth, because myth is the language of the infinite. The language that takes us beyond. It is not controlled by the letter, by the left hemisphere of the brain, or by institutions. It is story—deep, radical story. Stories of the people, and for the people, that the people may live. All the people, not just the two-legged people. All earth people. Doctrine without myth kills, just as Paul says the letter kills. *Rigor mortis* (the rigor of death) sets in when church or any other tradition prefers control over myth, or whenever it has sucked myth out of its doctrine. Doctrine with myth gives life that is spirit. As it says in Deuteronomy: "I have set before you life and prosperity, death and doom . . . Choose life, then, that you and your descendants may live" (Dt 30:15,19).

Now to the question: Is there a Christian myth for today? There are a lot of them. All of our doctrines, essentially, are myths, with powerful energy to them. I will lay out just a few.

The Doctrine of the Cosmic Christ

Yale church historian Jaroslav Pelikan observed that the Enlightenment deposed the cosmic Christ and made the quest for the historical Jesus necessary. What is the cosmic Christ? I ran into a fellow a year ago and he said, "I'm so excited about your cosmic Christ book; I've read it twice. But I have one question: What's a cosmic Christ?" What a moment of humility that was. Gregory of Nazianzen of the fourth century said, "Christ exists in all things that are." That's cosmic Christ. Teilhard de Chardin in our century said, "Christ is in the heart of the tiniest atom." That's cosmic Christ. It's this "thing" inside things. A contemporary physicist in Germany has just demonstrated that there are light photons in every atom in the universe. The First Letter of John says, "God is light" (1:5). Now science and theology are coming together again. Christ is the light in all beings, in every galaxy, every star, every atom, every whale, every drop of water; everyone contains the Christ, the light of the world. Hildegarde of Bingen in the twelfth century said, "Every creature is a glittering, glistening mirror of God." Being a mirror of God, being an image of God, this is the cosmic Christ tradition. It is an absolutely basic doctrine in western religion, in Judaism as well as Christianity, but we lost sight of it especially during this anthropocentric Newtonian era when we were told that the world was a machine and not a mirror of the divine.

There is a wonderful rabbinical saying: "Every time a human walks down the street, they are preceded by hosts of angels who sing out, 'Make way, make way, make way for the image of God.'" That's the cosmic Christ tradition. It is a powerful myth, absolutely essential for healing our society plagued by its self hatred and its shame-based religion by its inability to find the life that is inside. As Anne Wilson-Schaef says, "The essence of addiction is the external referencing of our flight from the mystic inside." The cosmic Christ tradition shows us we are all mystics. As Meister Eckhart said, "When I floated out of the creator," (meaning when he was born), "all creatures stood up and said, 'Behold, here is God.'" Those creatures were correct. This is good theology. We are God's sons and daughters as Eckhart said, but we do not realize it yet. It is as Jesus said, "You shall love your neighbors as yourself" (Mt 22:39). If we can't find the Divine within and among us, it won't be found. The cosmic Christ is a very powerful myth.

Mother Earth Crucified

The story of Mother Earth (Gaia) is part of the cosmic Christ tradition. Mother Earth is being crucified, yet she rises daily. The paschal mystery is re-enacted in Gaia. I recently celebrated the sacred triduum, the crucifixion/resurrection story, focusing on the theme of Mother Gaia. On Good Friday we prayed the stations of the cross outdoors; a small group created each station of the Crucified One today. There was a station for AIDS. There was a station where they hung a picture of the earth, and pounded nails into it. The people that created this station were so moved by their experience, which was accompanied by much crying and wailing, that afterwards they remained in silence for thirty minutes. Resetting our rituals of the paschal mystery into a Gaia context is of tremendous power today. In her wounds, in the wounds of the Christ in Gaia today, there is redemption, because by our entering the wounds instead of denying them, we change our ways. This is how we get converted.

The wonderful contemporary poet, philosopher, potter and painter, M.C. Richards, has written a poem called "Deep Ecology." The poem is a response to two sentences: one from my book on the cosmic Christ and a sentence from Julian of Norwich. From *The Coming of the Cosmic Christ:* "I believe the appropriate symbol of the cosmic Christ become incarnate in Jesus, is of Jesus as Mother Earth crucified, yet rising daily." And from Julian of Norwich: "Jesus is our true mother, in whom we are endlessly carried and out of whom we will never come." Responding to these thoughts, M.C. Richards writes:

> Christ's blood is green
>   in the branches,
> blue in the violet.
>   Her bright voice
> laughs in the night wind.
>   The big nova swells
> in her breast.
>   Christ suckles us
> with spring sap and
>   spreads earth under our feet.
>
> Oh, she loves us,
> feeds us, tricks us with
> her triple ways:
> calls us soul,
> calls us body and spirit.
> Calls us to her bed."[1]

Peter Russell, a British scientist known for his writings on the global brain, ends a recent article by observing, "The root of our environmental crisis is an inner spiritual aridity. Any truly wholistic environmental policy must include this in its approach: we need not only conduct research in the physical and biological sciences, we also need to explore the psychological and more sacred sciences." He calls for another Manhattan Project (the one that produced the atomic bomb), but this one focusing on human consciousness. Just as fifty years ago we put so much energy into exploding the power of the atom, so, he thinks, we need to put real energy into awakening consciousness. He points to St. Francis of Assisi and to Theresa of Avila, who demonstrate, he says, that in all of us there is immense mystical consciousness that is going untapped. His point is that our educational systems, our worship systems, even our psychological systems, often crucify the mystic in us. That mystic lamb. I've always been struck by how the Scriptures call Christ the Lamb and not a sheep. Why? The *puer*? The child? Was it the child that was killed on the cross? All empires crucify the child. Our academic establishment is still doing that.

We don't give the Lamb its place to play in the universe, and that is what Jesus meant, I think, about being good shepherds. Shepherd the Lamb inside, the child inside.

The Return of the Goddess and the Green Man in Our Time

Of course, the goddess came roaring through Western Christianity in the twelfth century in the figure of Mary. Within one hundred and twenty-five years in France alone, five hundred cathedrals the size of Chartres were dedicated to Mary, the mother goddess of Christianity. When the goddess comes, creativity comes. This awakening in the twelfth century was a cosmological awakening. Here is an indication. The word "cathedral" was invented. The word *cathedra* in Latin means chair or throne. In the twelfth century that throne was for Mary. It was the throne the goddess sits in. Ninety-nine percent of today's Roman Catholics would say that a cathedral has a chair in it for the bishop to sit in. Notice how we have anthropocentrized, clericalized, and patriarchized the whole thing; no wonder there's so little power there. Let me make it clear: a cathedral is not a cathedral because the bishop sits there. It is a cathedral because it is a place where the goddess of the universe rules. When our times rediscover that, we will rediscover the power of worship.

The green man, who is a very ancient figure, was also present in twelfth-century mythology and was incorporated into Christian cosmology. In medieval cathedrals he is usually pictured as having a wreath as a beard. Hildegarde of Bingen who was part of the twelfth-century renaissance said, "Christ is the green figure itself who brings lush greenness to shriveled and wilted people and institutions." That's a pretty nice image. Christ, the green man bringing lush greenness to our shriveled and wilted people and institutions.

What is a cathedral for our time? It is not a church building—it is earth itself. It is Gaia. Not everyone heard this, but do you know that what really got the Eastern European countries marching for democracy in recent years was the following slogan: "Better die of bullets than of choking." It was the ecological crucifixion of the earth in their countries that gave Eastern Europeans the courage to get up and be counted and to take the risk of being killed by bullets because they knew they would not survive otherwise. Now when we so-called "First Worlders" wake up and come alive to the issues of the earth we will produce a drama and a ritual that will be just as rich as that produced by the so-called "Second World."

If you examine the last one hundred and twenty-five years in the west, you will see that the escatological torch, the vision for the poor and the oppressed, has been Marxist. The rest of the world has been responding to it, reacting against it. Now that dynamic has passed and that torch is out. Yet Marx's analysis of capitalism still has much power to it. I believe the torch of the nineties, and of the next century, is earth itself. Earth can wake up the young; it can wake up the rich and the poor, together—east, west, north, and south, male and female. Earth contains the kind of power that the cathedral held in the twelfth century, when building a cathedral got everyone involved, and involved to perform what is essentially an impractical act.

Sedes Sapientiae, the Seat of Wisdom

To speak of wisdom is to speak of origins. And to speak of origins is to speak of our creation stories. We have a new creation story today. Who is we? We is the whole planet. Every race, every ethnic group, every religious group is being tuned into this story, because it is coming from science. It is found in India, China, Russia, Africa, the Americas, and Europe. The new creation story says that things began about eighteen billion years ago as a fire smaller than a pinhead; it expanded over seven hundred and fifty thousand years, giving birth to the elements of this universe, from which everything has been born and through which everything is connected. We now know that the universe had to be eight billion years long historically for us to be here, and it had to be one trillion galaxies big. I just love that thought because it means to me that the universe knew it was birthing this very, very risky species, the human species. Into this animal it was going to pour in the divine power of creativity and it said, "Let's stand back and watch this one; let's give ourselves one trillion galaxies of space to absorb what might happen." These are big stories.

Creation stories are what keep tribes together. Now at this very moment in history when we are within ten years of killing Gaia, we are also being gifted with such a story. Erich Jantsch, a physicist, in his important book *The Self-Organizing Universe* says, "God is the mind of the universe." What he means by mind is a dynamic which self evolves. In this respect, he says, "all natural history is also the history of mind." "Up to now," he says, "this all-embracing image of the universe was only understood by mystics." Now, he says, "I can talk about it as a scientist; it will enter more fully into and come closer to everyday life." And so the new creation ideas coming from science are deeply mystical, and therefore, mythical.

These ideas link up with the best things happening in scripture study today. The most important thing that is happening in New Testament study is the rediscovery (and it took feminist theologians to find this again) that the first name given to Jesus in the writings of the New Testament is Sophia, or Lady Wisdom. The Pauline writings, the oldest in the New Testament have it; you find it throughout John's Gospel; you find it, in fact, in all four Gospels. Lady Wisdom, the incarnation of Wisdom, is the way in which the first generation of Christians understood the historical Jesus. This fact has been covered up. In seminary courses on the Gospel of John students are taught a theology about Logos, the male hellenistic principal; but this theology is second-generation thinking. It was developed to place some parameters on the wisdom material I just mentioned. But, you see, the emergence of wisdom from the biblical tradition today, along with the emergence of wisdom from science, is one more sign of how awe abounds. Dr. Beverly Rubik, when talking about the new creation story as a physicist, says that the universe is just too awesome for things to be explained by chance any more. There is an anthropic principal we get from science which says that the universe has been a set up for life from the very beginning. There has been a conspiracy; decisions were made in the first second of the original fireball that were on behalf of life on this planet. She says it is clear that we are all biolasers, radiating light to one another in the universe; we are bioradiant beings. This awakening to wisdom that is coming from our new origin story marks one of the great moments in the development of human consciousness and it is happening today right under our feet.

Easter

Easter, resurrection, eggs. Think eggs, think new birth, think of the rolling away of stones by angels. Think of how we are in tombs; we are entombed in our Enlightenment paradigms, in our mechanistic universe, in our anthropocentrism. We are being visited by angels today who are rolling away the stones, opening up the universe again to us, showing us the intrinsic mystery of all things, including the mystery of our own bodies. To know that every element in your body was birthed in a supernova explosion five and a half billion years ago is to take your power back, and to quit projecting it onto stars, the stars of Hollywood, the stars of Washington, D.C., the stars of the Vatican. We are all stardust, literally. We are royal persons; this is an ancient theological tradition. That is why Jesus said that we are living in the kingdom and queendom of God; and he directed this message especially to the poor and the simple ones. We are royal persons and the proof of it is that we are literally stardust. Don't let anyone treat you differently. If we allow that to happen we become part of addictive systems, we become co-dependent. Jesus taught that *all* are sons and daughters of God.

The resurrection story also enables us to overcome the fear of death. The psychiatrist Otto Rank, who remained faithful to Judaism all his life, nevertheless said that the most revolutionary idea that has ever occurred to humans, was the teaching of Jesus and Paul about the resurrection. In Rank's work with artists and other creative people he found that the greatest obstacle to creativity is the fear of death. He said that what Jesus did was to "democratize the soul," that is, to move the idea of eternal life away from pyramids, and pharaohs and kings, and help us realize that everybody has resurrection in them and therefore need never fear death. Without the fear of death we can get on with living. And what living means, essentially, is to create. God is the creator who says "choose life not death."

Aquinas has a particular treatment of the resurrection that I have never seen in any other theologian's work. He talks about two resurrections: the first resurrection and the second resurrection. He says the first resurrection is our waking up in this lifetime. He invokes all the resurrection texts of the Scriptures. He says, "wake from your sleep!" Waking from our sleep, that is what the first resurrection is about. The second resurrection is about what happens after this lifetime. But he calls us to pay attention to that mystical invitation to the first resurrection. I think the real question is: Is there life *before* death? Aquinas says that we must try to rise spiritually from the soul's death to a life of justice. He quotes Ephesians, "Arise thou who sleep, arise from the dead and Christ shall enlighten thee." The idea that resurrection means arising from our sleepiness is a very powerful myth and is badly needed today. We can and do rise from death often. As a species we must do this in our lifetime. In our lifetime we have to change our ways, and that can only happen by rising from the dead.

Another dimension of the resurrection myth is the ascension of Christ. Now to most people the ascension means that Jesus went up into the sky, into heaven. But as Buckminister Fuller said, "Anyone today who uses the words "up" and "down" is five hundred years out of date." There is no up and down in a curved surface; we live in a curved universe. What does the ascension mean? It means Jesus went out, the Christ went out. Out into all one trillion galaxies. No other generation has known how far out Christ had to go to take the news and the grace to all corners, to all the atoms. Remember that when the people saw the risen Christ they did not say, "We've seen the historical Jesus! We've seen the historical Jesus!" They didn't say that. They said rather, "We've seen the risen Lord." Lord is a cosmic Christ title. They saw the cosmic Christ with wounds. Don't forget the wounds. That is an essential element in the story, and *there* is found the power. This element is what Christianity brings to the cosmic Christ traditions around the world: that the Divine One does not come just as a light in all things, but also as the wounds in all things. In this universe, to live is to be wounded, and even when God passes through, God gets wounded.

The Exodus Story, the Story of Liberation

This story is alive and well wherever people are genuinely involved in liberating events such as those people in base ecclesial communities in Latin America, where in our lifetime and on this continent, blood is flowing. Blood is flowing in quantities that have not been seen since the first century in Rome. We have to take energy from these martyrs, Oscar Romero, the Jesuit priests, their housekeepers, the women, many of this country, raped and murdered by armed forces that our country is still paying more than four and a half million dollars a day to support.

Tens of thousands of peasant leaders, farmers, union organizers, have been killed in Central America and in Brazil. During the sabbatical that the Vatican so graciously granted me two years ago, I visited Latin America. In Brazil I had a wonderful meeting with Bishop Pedro Casaldaliga (a beautiful bishop, also silenced by the Vatican), a poet and mystic, who works with the Amazon Indians. When I was there, about eighty of his co-workers who labored with the Indians and with people defending the rain forest were gathered together for a week. One night they celebrated a liturgy dedicated to our martyrs, and everyone went up and lit one candle and recited the names of two persons in their base communities whom they had known personally who had been tortured and killed. Afterwards, one man told me that the hard part was limiting the names to two: "I could name at least ten off the top of my head," he said. I tell you this story, because we North Americans need to learn courage. The Latin Americans are learning the new cosmology that is coming out of North America. (Leonardo Boff told me he is learning English to study the new cosmology.) But we have to learn courage from the Latin Americans. It is in all of us to be brave.

Do you know that is what true prayer is? I learned this in a vision quest I made with native Americans in Spokane and Seattle. One thing they taught me was this: in their culture, in their religion, they don't teach that God makes evil spirits, but rather that humans do and human institutions do. Furthermore, the door to letting evil spirits into the heart is fear. Good prayer, strong prayer is standing up to fear; it is developing a strong heart. We need this strong prayer in our time. Not prayer out of books, not prayer with our eyes, not prayer that you need to be literate to do, but strong prayer that makes us both powerful in our joy and delight, and powerful in our struggle. The Latin American church currently uses a word "ecclesiogenesis," meaning "to birth church."

A young man came up to me a year ago and said, "I can't decide whether to stay in the church or leave it." I said, "There's a third option. Birth church. Ecclesiogenesis." This birthing of church is a powerful myth. John XXIII called upon it when he launched the Second Vatican Council by calling for a new Pentecost. We have to listen to the spirit, and birth church at base communities, especially where we do our work.

The Holy, Catholic Church

In the Nicene Creed we say, "I believe in the holy, catholic church." Notice what we do *not* say. We do not say, "I believe in the holy Roman catholic church." Now there are times when the Roman Church is closer to being catholic than at other times. To believe in the holy, catholic church, we have to believe in ecumenism. We have to draw forth riches from all world religions and certainly from all Christian denominations. No one of them is owner of this archetype of being catholic or holy.

Worship

Worship is a microcosmic experience of the macrocosmic awe and wonder. What is missing in ninety-nine percent of white folks' worship is the cosmos, both micro and macro. White folks' worship is too anthropocentric. In many ways worship has to start over again in the west. The older I get, the more I realize that our Christian doctrines and our major religious rituals are not really about Jesus, not about something two thousand years old, but about the cosmos. The eucharist in the Christian tradition names a cosmic law: everything in the universe eats and gets eaten. Whole galaxies are born, do their work, and die. They give themselves away. Just like Jesus did. Whole species go the same way. The paschal mystery is a cosmic law about the life, death, and resurrection of all beings in the universe. I think we could say that the law of sacrifice is the eucharistic law of the universe. The Greek word *eucharistia* means "thank you." Eucharist is an act of gratitude for the many sacrifices made on the part of the universe on our behalf.

Our Being God's Sons and Daughters

When Jesus said, "Be you compassionate, as your creator in heaven is compassionate," he was calling us to be who we are and to exercise our divine capacity for compassion. For the Jew, compassion is the ultimate moral attribute of the Divine One. The sense of dignity (and the sense of responsibility) that comes from believing that we are truly God's sons and daughters, that there is divinity flowing through us, needs to be celebrated. This belief is called the third article of faith in our tradition. The first article is creation, the second redemption, and the third, our divinization, or our sanctification. We often do not get around to dealing with that third article. As a matter of fact in the west we have been so worried about sin and redemption (the second article) that we don't even pay attention to the first article. People today want and need to hear about their sanctification. Young people want to be told the *Good* News. They want to be told that life is not just about shopping malls but that we are here on this earth to do divine things, to carry on the divine work. John's epistle says that we are God's sons and daughters. That is who we are. I think the left brain ideology that has dominated our world for so long hardens our heart, trivializes our faith, and prevents us from hearing the big news that the young person in all of us yearns to hear.

The Four Paths of Telling Our Story,
the Four Paths in Creation Spirituality

This is the story of the hero and the shero, the story of the saintly journey that Joseph Campbell said each one of us must take. Campbell pointed out that figuratively one has to leave one's village with all its comforts and securities, and even its binding traditional ways to go on such a journey. It is a dangerous adventure, requiring the courage to let go of the past, with its truths, goals, and gifts, and to die to the world in order to come to birth from within. The ultimate aim of the quest must be neither release nor ecstasy for oneself, but the wisdom and power to serve others.

This happens when we travel through the four paths of Creation Spirituality. The first path is a journey of joy and delight in the wonder of existence itself. The second path is a journey through darkness when the heart breaks open, and power of a different kind flows forth. The third path is a journey into creativity, to awaken our own capacity as artists who can give birth to our own images. And the fourth path of the journey is the struggle for transformation and justice marked by compassion and healing. Campbell says myths are stories that put us in touch with our experience of being alive. They tell us what the experience of aliveness is. I believe these four paths can contribute to that experience and that, in fact, they represent the paschal mystery going on in our personal lives, and in our group lives.

The Trinity

Fundamentalism is alive and well in all the world religions, including Christianity. The trinitarian myth can rescue us from fundamentalism. How? It does so by reminding us that God is not only the redeemer, but is also the creator who is panentheistically present, omnipresent in all things. God is also spirit, and no one controls spirit. The Second Vatican Council in its document on non-Christian religions said that the Spirit has always worked through all religions and in all cultures. Notice that the council didn't say that Jesus has always worked through all cultures, but that the Spirit has. The doctrine of Trinity, I think, is a very important doctrine for our time.

Every living doctrine is a myth. Living doctrines are those that awaken new myths and connect us to old myths. That is their power. Fortunately, we are moving into an era of great remythologizing. Our ancestors, the communion of saints, is urging us on. Can we get the adventure back? Can we train young people for adventure? Surely we cannot depend on the current seminary system which has drained us of so much power to offer leadership in this important task. It is rare, unfortunately, to find mysticism alive in seminaries around the country. We have to ask whether seminaries are capable of producing heroes and sheroes to bring forth the hero and shero, the saint, in every one of us.

No, I believe that grassroots leadership is the future. Grassroots leadership. I experience this daily, frankly, in the work I do at the Institute in Culture and Creation Spirituality, where more and more people are responding to their vocation to be leaders, be they in their sixties or their twenties, whatever their religious background and whatever their profession. Many people have been called by Gaia, and by the Divine One to become spiritual directors in the broadest sense of the word. Their humanity has been awakened and they have become more than they were. Here one sees the invitation and the power of myth. Christians have a lot of them.

Concluding her great work, *The Interior Mansions,* Theresa of Avila says, "I've only spoken of seven rooms in your soul. But, in fact, there are millions of rooms, every one of them containing labyrinths and fountains and gardens and precious jewels." I've only touched on a few Christian doctrines. There are many, many more. Everyone of them contains labyrinths and fountains, gardens and jewels. But to imbibe these, we have to let go of the letter that kills; we have to approach them with heart and body and with the right hemisphere of the brain. We must take off our shoes. We cannot enter without letting go, without undergoing. Are we eager to make this journey together? Is our generation eager to make this journey together? Are we eager to present the young ones with a spiritual adventure? I close with a sentence from Thomas Aquinas, "The experience of God must not be restricted to the few or to the old."

NOTE

1. M.C. Richards, *Imaging Inventing Yellow: New and Selected Poems* (Station Hill Press, 1991)

Contributors

Dr. William Dinges is Associate Professor in the Department of Religion and Religious Education at The Catholic University of America. He has written extensively in the areas of religion and culture, the sociology of religion and American religious history. He has a special interest in the impact of Joseph Campbell's thought on the American religious landscape.

Rev. Peter E. Fink, S.J. is Associate Professor of Sacramental Theology at Weston School of Theology in Cambridge, Massachusetts where he leads a seminar on Joseph Campbell. He is the author of numerous articles and editor of the *New Dictionary of Sacramental Worship* (Liturgical Press/Glazier).

Rev. Matthew Fox, O.P. is the Founding Director of the Institute in Culture and Creation Spirituality at Holy Names College in Oakland, California. He is a popular lecturer and the author of twelve books including *The Coming of the Cosmic Christ* (Harper & Row) and *Original Blessing: A Primer in Creation Spirituality* (Bear and Company).

Rev. Brian O. McDermott, S.J. is Associate Professor of Systematic Theology at Weston School of Theology in Cambridge, Massachusetts. He received his Doctorate from the University of Nijmegen, Holland, and is the author of *Word Become Flesh: Dimensions of Christology* (Liturgical Press/Glazier) and numerous other publications on Christology.

Ms. Gertrud Mueller Nelson, a native of Cologne, Germany, has been involved in Montessori education, studied art in Germany and attended the C.G. Jung Institute in Zurich. A popular speaker on Christian ritual and liturgical celebration, she is the author of *To Dance with God* (Paulist Press), and *Here All Dance Free: Stories to Heal the Wounded Feminine* (Doubleday).

Dr. Dennis L. O'Connor has explored eastern and western wisdom traditions for thirty years. He received his Doctorate from Cornell University, and serves as author, consultant, workshop presenter, and instructor at Georgetown University, Virginia Theological Seminary, and the Servant Leadership School on issues related to the work of Joseph Campbell.

Dr. Robert A. Segal, is Associate Professor of Religious Studies at Louisiana State University. He is the author of *Joseph Campbell: An Introduction* (New American Library) and many scholarly and critical articles on myth and ritual and the works of Campbell, Jung, Turner, and Eliade.

Brother David Steindl-Rast, O.S.B., born in Vienna, Austria, has been a monk of Mount Saviour Monastery in New York State since 1953 and currently lives at Immaculate Heart Hermitage, Big Sur, California. He holds a Ph.D. from the Psychological Institute at the University of Vienna. After twelve years of formal training in the 1500 year old Benedictine monastic tradition Brother David received permission to practice Zen with Buddhist masters. An international lecturer who spends most of the year in seclusion, Brother David has written *Gratefulness, the Heart of Prayer* (Paulist Press).

Ms. Beverley Zabriskie, C.S.W., NCPsyA., is a Jungian analyst in practice in New York City. She is a member of the New York and International Associations for Analytical Psychology, and is on the faculty of the New York C.G. Jung Institute. She has served on the boards of the Institute, the C.G. Jung Foundation, the editorial board of the journal *Quadrant*, and the National Association for the Advancement of Psychoanalysis, of which she is past president. She has taught and lectured extensively on Egyptian mythology and the imagery of alchemy.

Rev. Lawrence J. Madden, S.J., editor, is Director of The Georgetown Center for Liturgy, Spirituality and the Arts. He received his doctorate in liturgy from the University of Trier, Germany, and has served on the faculties of Georgetown University, The Catholic University of America, and the Washington Theological Union. He is a frequent speaker and author on topics of liturgy and spirituality.